TOWARDS AN ETHICS
OF AUTISM

Towards an Ethics of Autism

A Philosophical Exploration

Kristien Hens

https://www.openbookpublishers.com

ISBN Paperback: 9781800642300
ISBN Hardback: 9781800642317
ISBN Digital (PDF): 9781800642324
ISBN Digital ebook (epub): 9781800642331
ISBN Digital ebook (mobi): 9781800642348
ISBN XML: 9781800642355
DOI: 10.11647/OBP.0261

Cover image: Photo by Mika Baumeister on Unsplash at https://unsplash.com/photos/40HCUdMcHiw
Cover design by Anna Gatti.

Contents

Acknowledgements

This book is the result of ten years of philosophical and ethical explorations of autism. During that period, I spoke to many people, colleagues, students, autism professionals, parents of autistic children, and, last but not least, autistic people themselves. Not only did these conversations help me to think about autism with more nuance, but they also helped me think about philosophy and ethics in a more grounded way. Much of what I now believe to be true, both in ontology and ethics, is the result of my grappling with the many meanings of autism and appreciating the importance of the autistic experience. So my gratitude goes out to all the people I met on the way.

I want to thank the people from Open Book Publishers for their professional handling of this book: Alessandra Tosi, Lucy Barnes, Anna Gatti, Laura Rodriguez. I would also like to thank the anonymous reviewers who read the book's first version: your comments were spot on, and I enjoyed rewriting the book with your suggestions.

I would also like to thank the people from LAuRes (Leuven Autism Research) for welcoming me into their group and giving me a taste of the many aspects of clinical and fundamental research into autism. Thanks also to people from Autism Ethics for exciting workshops and philosophical discussions.

Raymond Langenberg, Susan Langenberg and Fleur Beyers from Campus Gelbergen offered great inspiration and help in writing the Dutch book, of which this book is a rewritten translation.

A special thanks to my colleagues Katrien Schaubroeck, Ilse Noens, Daniela Cutas, Anna Smajdor, Jean Steyaert, and Andreas De Block. You are colleagues in the truest sense of the word!

The ideas in this book formed the gist of my project proposal, which has received funding from the European Research Council (ERC) under the European Union's Horizon 2020 research and innovation programme (grant agreement No 804881). This grant allowed me to create my team, *NeuroEpigenEthics*. I could not have developed many of the ideas in this book without the input of all its former and current team members. Eman Ahmed, Jo Bervoets, Delphine Jacobs, Laura Mattys, Lisanne Meinen, Emma Moormann, Gert-Jan Vanaken, Leni Van Goidsenhoven: you are all stars. Thank you for a fantastic experience!

David, Roman, Aaron & Isaak: I spend too much time writing behind my computer, I know. You are what matters.

Prologue

Dynamics and Ethics of Autism

This is a book about the meanings, experiences and dynamics of autism.

My initial interest in autism began ten years ago. As a bioethicist who had written a PhD on pediatric biobanks, I was interested in the ethics of genetic research and genetic diagnostics of autism. These practices raise several questions in traditional biomedical ethics, such as what genetic findings should genetic counsellors convey to their clients, and are genetic 'risk' factors[1] for autism a good reason to opt for reproductive techniques such as in vitro embryo testing? Moreover, back in those days, and still today, public discourse on autism often centred around whether or not there are too many diagnoses of autism. Children with an autism diagnosis, previously scarce, were now to be found in every classroom. Some commentators have argued that this reflects the way that we pathologise and medicalise atypical behaviour. At the same time, parents of autistic children have often criticised this view, as they consider it a denial of the genuine challenges they and their child face. I soon realised that it is impossible to answer these ethical questions without reflecting carefully on the concept of autism itself. It seemed self-evident that when investigating questions about autism, we should first identify precisely what we mean by it. If we suggest that there are now too many diagnoses, this might imply that we think that some of the children currently diagnosed do not actually have autism, and that diagnostic practices should be more stringent. If

---

1   I have put 'risk' between quotation marks here, as I do not consider autism to be something that you risk. As I shall argue in chapter five, I consider disability to be neutral with regards to its appreciation. In my own writings, I use 'elevated likelihood'.

   https://doi.org/10.11647/OBP.0261.13

we argue that autism is something that people can choose to prevent through reproductive techniques, we need to set the record straight on what is being prevented.

When we ask ourselves what it would look like to do good in relation to any subject, and more specifically, what good clinical practice is, we first need a notion of what we are talking about. When thinking about autism and psychiatric diagnosis in general, this is a complex task. The ontological status of psychiatric diagnosis is the subject of fierce debate, and autism in particular is much discussed. However, this is not primarily a book about the history of autism. Scholars have written many books on this topic,[2] and those looking for an overview of autism and its history can consult the resources listed in the footnotes.

In this book, I shall draw up an approach to conceptualizing autism that I think has ontological and ethical benefits, without attempting to close down the discussion about the essence of autism. I will use the term autism rather than the official and widely used Autism Spectrum Disorder (ASD), as the latter only covers some of the many meanings of autism. The reader should also be aware that I write this book from a Belgian perspective. In Belgium, diagnosis is still an essential first step in searching for answers and solutions related to autism, both in children and adults. Clinicians here do not often prescribe extensive behavioural therapies such as Applied Behavioural Analysis (ABA), which are contested by many autistic people and which raise ethical questions of their own. I will therefore only dwell on them sporadically. In Belgium, a diagnosis is generally followed by support and services in school or the workplace and psychoeducation about autism. In this book I use the terms 'autistics' and 'autistic persons', rather than 'persons with autism',

---

2   See for example Roy Richard Grinker, *Unstrange Minds: Remapping the World of Autism* (Basic Books, 2008); Majia Holmer Nadesan, *Constructing Autism: Unravelling the 'Truth' and Understanding the Social* (London ; New York: Routledge, 2005); *The Autism Matrix: The Social Origins of the Autism Epidemic*, ed. by Gil Eyal (Cambridge, UK; Malden, MA: Polity, 2010); Bonnie Evans, *The Metamorphosis of Autism: A History of Child Development in Britain* (Manchester: Manchester University Press, 2017); Mitzi Waltz, *Autism. A Social and Medical History* (Basingstoke: Palgrave McMillan, 2013); Anne McGuire, *War on Autism: On the Cultural Logic of Normative Violence* (Ann Arbor: University of Michigan Press, 2016); Chloe Silverman, *Understanding Autism: Parents, Doctors, and the History of a Disorder* (Princeton: Princeton University Press, 2011); Steve Silberman, *Neurotribes: The Legacy of Autism and How to Think Smarter about People Who Think Differently* (Crows Nest: Allen & Uwin, 2015).

as the former is preferred by autistic people, at least in English-speaking countries.[3]

Autism professionals often talk about autism as something that is heterogenous, a spectrum. This suggests that autism can manifest itself in many different ways. For example, some autistic people have cognitive disabilities, and others have cognitive strengths. Some autistic people do not use verbal language, whereas others are comfortable with oral communication. Still, 'heterogeneity' or 'spectrum' suggests that autism itself is one thing. Over the years, I have acknowledged that autism is a multi-layered concept. It is polysemous. What a child psychiatrist means when they talk about autism can be something different from what a cognitive scientist means. It may be something different again from what it means for the autistic person.

In order to study the ethics of the genetics of autism, I first talked to several child psychiatrists. From their perspective, one important dimension of autism is that it is a psychiatric diagnosis based on assessing behaviour and functioning. 'To have autism', in this sense, means that you satisfy the criteria of a diagnostic manual, that a qualified diagnostician assesses the behaviour of the person in question through the lens of a behavioural diagnosis and that the person experiences sufficient impairment in day-to-day functioning to receive a diagnosis. The most frequently used diagnostic manual is the DSM (Diagnostic and Statistical Manual of Mental Disorders), currently in its fifth edition. For autism, the main difference between DSM-IV and DSM-5 is the dyad of behaviours in the latter, as shown in Table 1.[4] In DSM-IV, this was still a triad: it listed communication and social interaction as separate categories. DSM-5 gathers the earlier diagnoses of Asperger syndrome and PDD-NOS (Pervasive Developmental Disorder — Not Otherwise Specified) and some other conditions under 'Autism Spectrum Disorder'. Moreover, the authors of the DSM-5 have tried to approach the diagnosis in a more multi-dimensional way: different people with an autism diagnosis can exhibit a particular behaviour to a greater or lesser degree. Each characteristic might manifest at different levels of severity.

---

3   Lorcan Kenny et al., 'Which Terms Should Be Used to Describe Autism? Perspectives from the UK Autism Community', *Autism*, 2015, https://doi.org/10.1177/1362361315588200

4   American Psychiatric Association, *Diagnostic and Statistical Manual of Mental Disorders (Fifth Ed.)* (Arlington: American Psychiatric Publishing, 2013).

This dimensional approach does not take away from the fact that the diagnosis itself is still categorical: you either have autism or you do not have it; you cannot have it somewhat. We might ask ourselves how far a dimensional approach is compatible with the idea of a spectrum. A spectrum suggests a gradual transition between different types. In contrast, a dimensional system indicates that different people can have various aspects to a greater or lesser degree, and are difficult to pin down on a gradient. The Canadian philosopher of science Ian Hacking, whom we shall meet again in chapter ten, prefers to speak about a manifold.[5]

In the DSM-5, one of the criteria that must be fulfilled in order to qualify for a diagnosis of autism is that 'Symptoms cause clinically significant impairment in social, occupational, or other important areas of current functioning'. How much someone experiences such impairment can depend on properties intrinsic to the individual. For example, your IQ can be an asset or it can make certain symptoms more challenging. How much you suffer from sensory hypersensitivity can depend on how your brain functions. The level of dysfunction also depends on the context. For example, a person in a quiet and structured environment may perform better than someone in a chaotic environment.

Moreover, functioning is dependent on the values of both the assessor and the assessed. Specific characteristics of one's life, such as not having many friends or having a preoccupation with certain topics, might be considered dysfunctional from an outsider's perspective. Nevertheless, the person may be perfectly happy. In this book, I do not use the frequently used labels 'high-functioning' (or 'mild') autism or 'low-functioning' (or 'severe') autism. These terms, first of all, presuppose that we can quickly grasp the essence of autism and that, based on this essence, you can decide whether it is more or less present. For a phenomenon such as autism, this might never be possible. Moreover, these terms suggest that the challenges of the 'high-functioning' autistic person—often associated with the stereotypical image of the highly gifted person with Asperger syndrome—are less than those of the person with an intellectual disability. If we consider the experiences of autistic persons with a wide range of characteristics, these subdivisions may turn out to be naive and even discriminatory.

---

5   Ian Hacking, 'Humans, Aliens & Autism', *Daedalus*, 138:3 (2009), 44–59, https://doi. org/10.1162/daed.2009.138.3.44

If the DSM-5 is strictly followed, someone who satisfies all behavioural criteria but who can successfully integrate these characteristics into their life without experiencing impairments in their everyday life will not qualify for a diagnosis of autism. This implies that, in the context of scientific research, one could screen a population for autistic characteristics, but the appearance of such characteristics would not straightforwardly mean that a person should be diagnosed with autism in the clinical sense. Autism or Autism Spectrum Disorder is therefore a clinical diagnosis based on assessing what is best for a person with a particular need for clinical help.

Besides the DSM, there are other classificatory systems such as ICD-10, the classificatory system for diseases created by the WHO (World Health Organization). The latter also mentions challenges in social functioning and communication, as well as restricted interests, as characteristics of autism. Diagnosticians working with either system use instruments for behavioural diagnoses, such as ADOS-2 (Autism Diagnostic Observation Scale), to measure whether individuals satisfy the diagnostic criteria.[6] The DSM further mentions that autistic behaviour has to be present early in development to qualify for a diagnosis, whereas ICD-10 states that autism lasts throughout a person's lifetime. They both mention that there is no cure, but treatment can help. They also state that treatments include behaviour and communication therapies and medicines to control symptoms, and that starting treatment as early as possible is important. The emphasis in ICD-10 on the fact that autism is quasi-innate and lifelong is fascinating: in chapter one, we shall describe how one of the early investigators of autism, Hans Asperger, stated this, but that another early investigator, Leo Kanner, suggests in a 1943 paper that some evolution is possible. Still, this emphasis on the innate and lifelong nature of autism indicates that it is different to—perhaps even more *real* than—a mere psychiatric diagnosis or a clinical presentation that we use to describe the challenges of a child or adult to guide further treatment and support. Autism as an idea seems to refer to a particular neurobiological reality. It looks as if autism is less susceptible to change

---

6   Johnny L. Matson, *Handbook of Assessment and Diagnosis of Autism Spectrum Disorder* (New York: Springer International Publishing, 2016); Adam McCrimmon and Kristin Rostad, 'Test Review: Autism Diagnostic Observation Schedule, Second Edition (ADOS-2) Manual (Part II): Toddler Module', *Journal of Psychoeducational Assessment*, 32:1 (2014), 88–92, https://doi.org/10.1177/0734282913490916

than a mood disorder such as depression. Maybe autism is even an atypical way of being in the world, which is, in principle, equally as good as what is considered the typical or even normal way. Perhaps, when we think about autism, we more readily conjure up this more essentialist meaning, rather than the clinical meaning.

This second dimension of autism, that of a neurobiological reality, is apparent in the many research projects that seek to find the cause of autism. Taking a clinical diagnosis as a starting point, they seek to find the underlying gene or neurological functioning to explain autistic behaviour. This approach is not only popular with researchers, but autistic people also often acknowledge that they consider autism to have a biological explanation. Around 2016, researcher Raymond Langenberg and I conducted a phenomenological study about the meaning of a diagnosis of autism for adults.[7] We interviewed twenty-one people about their recent diagnosis. We asked them how they experienced the diagnostic process and their lives before and after the diagnosis. We had noticed how—after a long period of feeling different and often of suffering—they welcomed the diagnosis. Throughout their lives, some of our respondents had received several other diagnoses; for example, borderline personality disorder (this was more common among the women) or obsessive-compulsive personality disorder. Many felt, however, that the diagnosis of autism was the correct one and corresponded to who they were. Some pointed out the importance of finally knowing that their challenges related to how their brain functioned, as this meant these challenges would not be overcome if they simply tried hard enough. This realisation gave them peace of mind: such an effort had cost many of them a great deal of energy without much benefit. At the same time, they sometimes struggled with the reductionist implications of the diagnosis of autism, and its neurobiological status. They often felt that they were more than what was implied by the label and what it caused some of the people around them to assume.

Our conclusion in this study was that autism as a concept worked for the people we interviewed. They experienced autism as real and situated in biology, unlike a personality disorder (such as borderline

---

7   Kristien Hens and Raymond Langenberg, *Experiences of Adults Following an Autism Diagnosis* (Cham: Palgrave Macmillan, 2018).

personality disorder), as people consider these to be mental disorders. Simultaneously, autism is heterogeneous to such an extent that people who are diagnosed do not have to coincide entirely with the diagnosis. People can pick out those aspects with which they identify. It seems that it is the idea that autism is real, in your brain and your genes, that allows people to accept it as a diagnosis. What we have learned in our research, by talking to people with a diagnosis of autism, with psychiatrists and with other autism professionals, is that autism is indeed real as a shared experience, as something that can be known as a phenomenon.

This book explores three central themes in thinking about autism that are ethically relevant. The approach is inspired by Karen Barad's ethico-onto-epistem-ology: the idea that a phenomenon cannot be separated from how we know and study it. This, in turn, is inextricably linked with ethical practice, which should never be a mere afterthought once the research has been done. This book, therefore, does not give ready-made answers to the ethical questions posed in the first paragraph. Instead, I hope to demonstrate that what we know and how we know things matters. I offer a way of looking at autism that may inspire ethical practices.

The first theme is that of the many meanings of autism. In part one, I shall describe different layers of meaning and their implications for the ethics of autism. The aim is not to reduce different dimensions to one true meaning but to engage with uncertainties inextricably linked to autism. Chapter one examines two seminal writings on autism, by Leo Kanner and Hans Asperger, and describes how, even in these writings, autism had different meanings. Chapter two tackles the issue of psychiatric diagnoses and what it means if someone is considered to be "psychiatrically ill'. Chapter three presents some cognitive explanatory models and their implications for meta-ethics and applied ethics. In chapter four, I examine sociological explanations for the rise and expansion of autism.

In part two, we shall investigate the importance of experience in understanding a phenomenon such as autism. This is inspired by standpoint epistemology, the idea that knowledge arises from a social position. Chapter five explores different models of disability and their application to autism. Chapter six introduces the concept of epistemic injustice and how many people have not taken the accounts of autistic people seriously for a long time. In chapter seven, I present some ideas from our interview study mentioned above. Chapter eight is an interlude about experiences of time and autism.

A recurrent theme in the book and discussions about autism, in general, is the importance of biology, more specifically of genes and neurology. Biology makes a phenomenon such as autism appear more concrete, less imagined. Simultaneously, associating something with genes or neurology also risks a reductionist and deterministic interpretation, which can lead to stigma. In part three, I pry apart the link between biology and such reductionism and suggest ways to look dynamically at biology. I formulate an alternative to, on the one hand, reductionist biological and cognitive explanations, and on the other hand, approaches that consider autism to be a mere social construct or even a fabrication. Chapter nine describes the dynamics of diagnoses, using, amongst others, the concept of looping effects devised by the philosopher of science Ian Hacking. Chapter ten contains descriptions of dynamic models of biology and human minds. Chapter eleven investigates the impact of ideas of genetics in the context of autism. In the epilogue, I suggest how the ideas presented in this book can shed new light on ethical questions surrounding autism.

Table 1: DSM-5 criteria for autism[8]

A. Persistent deficits in social communication and social interaction across multiple contexts, as manifested by the following, currently or by history.
   A1. Deficits in social-emotional reciprocity, ranging, for example, from abnormal social approach and failure of normal back-and-forth conversation; to reduced sharing of interests, emotions, or affect; to failure to initiate or respond to social interactions.
   A2. Deficits in nonverbal communicative behaviors used for social interaction, ranging, for example from poorly integrated verbal and nonverbal communication; to abnormalities in eye contact and body language or deficits in understanding and use of gestures; to a total lack of facial expressions and nonverbal communication.

---

8   DSM-5, p.109–10.

A3. Deficits in developing, maintaining, and understandings relationships, ranging, for example, from difficulties adjusting behavior to suit various social contexts; to difficulties in sharing imaginative play or in making friends; to absences of interest in peers.

B. Restricted, repetitive patterns of behavior, interests, or activities as manifested by **at least 2 of 4 symptoms** currently or by history.

B1. Stereotyped or repetitive motor movements, use of objects, or speech (e.g. simple motor stereotypes, lining up toys or flipping objects, echolalia, idiosyncratic phrases).

B2. Insistence on sameness, inflexible adherence to routines, or ritualized patterns of verbal or nonverbal behavior (e.g. extreme distress at small changes, difficulties with transitions, rigid thinking patterns, greeting rituals, need to take same route or eat same food everyday).

B3. Highly restricted, fixated interests that are abnormal in intensity or focus (e.g. strong attachment to or preoccupation with unusual objects, excessively circumscribed or preservative interest).

B4. Hyper- or hypo-reactivity to sensory input or unusual interest in sensory aspects of the environment (e.g. apparent indifference to pain/ temperature, adverse response to specific sounds or textures, excessive smelling or touching of objects, visual fascination with lights or movement).

C. Symptoms must be present in the early developmental periods (but may not become fully manifest until social demands exceed limited capacities, or may be masked by learned strategies in later life).

D. Symptoms cause clinically significant impairment in social, occupational, or other important areas of current functioning.

E. These disturbances are not better explained by intellectual disability (intellectual development disorder) or global development delay.

PART I: DIMENSIONS OF AUTISM

There ain't no answer.
There ain't going to be an answer.
There never has been an answer.
That's the answer.

Gertrude Stein

1. The Origins of Autism

In February 2020, three doctors stood trial for performing euthanasia in 2017 on Tine Nys, a thirty-eight-year-old woman with severe mental illness. Two months before her death, she had been diagnosed with autism. For the purposes of my account, it is irrelevant whether one approves of euthanasia for unbearable mental suffering, which is, in principle, legal in Belgium. The trial, the media, and the public reactions can shed some light on how autism has many meanings that we cannot merely reduce to one single meaning. For some commentators, many of them psychiatrists, it was bad practice to allow euthanasia to be performed a mere two months after the diagnosis. A psychiatric diagnosis, they said, is meant to provide a clinical image of a person's (dys)functioning, and as such, it is a starting point for clinical care. Two months is far too short to be able to assess the effectiveness of diagnosis and treatment. Others suggested that it is precisely this diagnosis that gave weight to the claim that Tine was suffering incurably and unbearably. Autism is, after all, a lifelong and incurable disorder, they argued. Still others, often parents of autistic children and autistic adults, took issue with the automatic link between autism and suffering. For them, autism is perhaps indeed something that one has from birth and until death, but it is by no means intrinsically and automatically linked with suffering and a worse life. All these different conceptions of autism: from a clinical presentation, a lifelong disorder to a neutral neurological difference, exist simultaneously. Nevertheless, the case of Tine Nys shows us that how we conceive of autism can have far-reaching normative consequences.

In this chapter, I shall investigate how at least three meanings of autism have existed from its inception as a concept and a term: autism as a (child) psychiatric disorder, autism as an innate and lifelong character trait, and autism as a developmental phenomenon. To do

 https://doi.org/10.11647/OBP.0261.01

so, I will return to what can be considered the original writings about autism: the English text from 1943 by Leo Kanner (1894–1981), 'Autistic Disturbances of Affective Contact'[1] and the German article from 1944 by Hans Asperger (1906–1980), 'Die "Autistischen Psychopathen" im Kindesalter'.[2] Both texts shed valuable light on what autism is and how it is seen today: on the one hand, a familial condition that is innate and probably lifelong, on the other hand, a developmental disorder that child psychiatrists can treat. Kanner's text anchored the concept of autism in the clinic, research, and the broader public. However, the word autism had already been used to refer to introverted children. For example, historical educational scientist Annemieke Van Drenth describes the work of Sister Gaudia (full name: Ida Frye (1909–2003). In the 1930s, Sister Gaudia was involved in the case of a boy called Siem.[3] She encountered the four-year-old Siem (a pseudonym) at the Paedological Institute in Nijmegen, which she founded. Siem had difficulties maintaining social contact, as well as language difficulties. Sister Gaudia suggested using the word 'autistic' to describe Siem's behaviour. Siem remained at the institute for eight years. After that, he was enrolled at a regular school and eventually took up a job as an accountant. However, for the actual origin of the term autism, we have to go back to the Swiss psychiatrist Eugen Bleuler (1857–1939), who used it to denote a specific symptom of schizophrenia: the withdrawal of reality.[4] In this context, it was primarily used to describe adults.

Leo Kanner has made history as the researcher who gave child psychiatry a jump-start in the United States with his description of autism. The work of the other founding father of current thinking about autism, Hans Asperger, was less well known for several decades, until Lorna Wing (1928–2014) discovered and translated it in the 1970s.

---

1   Leo Kanner, 'Autistic Disturbances of Affective Contact', *Acta Paedopsychiatrica*, 35:4 (1968), 100–36.

2   Hans Asperger, 'Die "Autistischen Psychopathen" im Kindesalter', *Archiv für Psychiatrie und Nervenkrankheiten*, 117:1 (1944), 76–136, https://doi.org/10.1007/BF01837709

3   Annemieke Van Drenth, 'Rethinking the Origins of Autism: Ida Frye and the Unraveling of Children's Inner World in the Netherlands in the Late 1930s', *Journal of the History of the Behavioural Sciences*, 54:1 (2018), 25–42, https://doi.org/10.1002/jhbs.21884

4   Bernard J. Crespi, 'Revisiting Bleuler: Relationship between Autism and Schizophrenia', *The British Journal of Psychiatry*, 196:6 (2010), 495–95, https://doi.org/10.1192/bjp.196.6.495

Asperger was subsequently discredited in 2018 because of the discovery of his links to the Nazi regime;[5] nonetheless, his work is essential to an understanding of the evolution of the concept of autism. It is worth noting that both Leo Kanner and Hans Asperger may have had the same influence for their conceptualisation of autism. Indeed, historical circumstances may have caused Kanner's and Asperger's predecessor, Georg Frankl, and his role in the early history of autism, to be forgotten. In a 2020 article, Filippo Muratori, Sara Calderoni, and Valeria Bizzari describe how Georg Frankl was a senior psychiatrist working in Vienna in the 1930s when Asperger was a postdoctoral researcher.[6] Frankl wrote an unpublished work on autism, in which he attributed the phenomenon to a child's poor understanding of the emotional content of words. It is very likely that Asperger knew of this work. Moreover, the authors describe how the well-known Russian psychiatrist Grunya Sukhareva had already published a paper on children with schizoid personality disorders in 1926. The description of the children was remarkably similar to the now famous description of autism by Hans Asperger. George Frankl, being Jewish, was forced to emigrate to the United States. It is certain that Leo Kanner knew Frankl and had read his work. Hence, the authors of the article argue, it is not the case that Frankl brought Asperger's ideas to the United States and to Leo Kanner as it is often believed. Instead, he may well have been the source of these ideas. Below, I will focus on the texts by Kanner and Asperger, because they are the best known in the field, and because they reflect different conceptualisations of autism that are relevant for my account. But the stories of Sister Gaudia, Grunya Sukhareva, and George Frankl should serve as a warning that reading history as a succession of individuals of genius and of founding fathers is wrong: many thinkers contribute to important ideas, and the reasons why some thinkers are installed in the canon cannot merely be attributed to merit. We can only guess how many great thinkers and ideas are forgotten by history because of their gender or because they belonged to a minority.

---

5   Herwig Czech, 'Hans Asperger, National Socialism, and "Race Hygiene" in Nazi-Era Vienna', *Molecular Autism*, 9 (2018), 29, https://doi.org/10.1186/s13229-018-0208-6

6   Filippo Muratori, Sara Calderoni and Valeria Bizzari, 'George Frankl: an undervalued voice in the history of autism', *Eur Child Adolesc Psychiatry* (2020), http://www.doi.org/10.1007/s00787-020-01622-4 (published online ahead of print).

Kanner's Autism:
Kick-Starting the Field of Child Psychiatry

Leo Kanner was a psychiatrist of Austrian descent, who founded the department of child psychiatry at the Johns Hopkins Hospital in Baltimore, Maryland, in the 1930s. He thus became the first official child psychiatrist in the United States. The history of autism as a child psychiatric condition starts in 1943 with Kanner's text, 'Autistic Disturbances of Affective Contact',[7] in which he describes eleven children who have one specific characteristic in common:

> The outstanding, "pathognomonic," fundamental disorder is the children's inability to relate themselves in the ordinary way to people and situations from the beginning of life. Their parents referred to them as having always been "self-sufficient"; "like in a shell"; "happiest when left alone"; "acting as if people weren't there"; "perfectly oblivious to everything about him"; "giving the impression of silent wisdom"; "failing to develop the usual amount of social awareness"; "acting almost as if hypnotised." This is not, as in schizophrenic children or adults, a departure from an initially present relationship; it is not a "withdrawal" from formerly existing participation. There is from the start an extreme autistic aloneness that, whenever possible, disregards, ignores, shuts out anything that comes to the child from the outside.[8]

Each person interested in autism should read this paper, if only to understand the context in which the discipline of child psychiatry was born. We find many characteristics still associated with autism: the children almost all mix up their pronouns and use 'you' rather than 'I' when they refer to themselves. Echolalia, repeating the words or sentences of an interlocutor, is mentioned several times. Kanner describes insistence on sameness to stress that these children are averse to change, a characteristic that is still frequently associated with autism today. Furthermore, we read that the children described by Kanner often experience sound and noise as disturbing and too intense. This hypersensitivity to sound is a characteristic that autistic persons often use to describe their experiences, but which has only just been taken up as a diagnostic criterion in DSM-5.

7　　Kanner, 'Autistic Disturbances of Affective Contact'.
8　　Ibid., p. 242.

Kanner wanted to distinguish the phenomenon of infantile autism from childhood schizophrenia. As mentioned before, he did not invent the term autism, but we have to look for its origin in theories about schizophrenia. Kanner, however, introduced a marked difference between what he calls autism and how the term was used in the context of schizophrenia. He suggested that autistic children, unlike children with childhood schizophrenia, do not withdraw from the world but are born with the condition. It is striking how he describes the way that these children, born autistic, in fact gradually come out, from themselves towards the world:

> While the schizophrenic tries to solve the problem by stepping out of the world of which he has been a part and with which he has been in touch, our children gradually compromise by extending cautious feelers into a world in which they have been total strangers from the beginning.[9]

Kanner describes the phenomenon as infantile autism. From this text alone, it is unclear what his prognosis was for the children he examined and what he would call the condition when it manifested in adults. He later described eleven adults that had been under his care as children.[10] Some of them had been sent to Devereux schools (schools for special education). Some had overcome some of their previous challenges. About Don, who was first seen by Kanner when he was five years old, Kanner wrote that in a letter from Don's mother, Don was described as working at a bank and having hobbies at age thirty-eight. Kanner and colleagues later researched how some of the children he had examined in his clinical practice fared once they were adults. He described how these children had learned social behaviour during adolescence and how many would earn degrees and find a job, although often they were loners.[11] Although Kanner suggested that these children often come from detached and individualistic families, and although he invented the term 'refrigerator mother', a label for mothers of autistic children, whose so-called coldness he considered to be the cause of

---

9   Ibid., p. 249.
10 Leo Kanner, 'Follow-up Study of Eleven Autistic Children Originally Reported in 1943', *Journal of Autism and Childhood Schizophrenia*, 1:2 (1971), 119–45.
11 Leo Kanner, Alejandro Rodriguez, and Barbara Ashenden, 'How Far Can Autistic Children Go in Matters of Social Adaptation?', *Journal of Autism and Childhood Schizophrenia*, 2:1 (1972), 9–33, https://doi.org/10.1007/BF01537624

their children's predicament, he did not state anywhere in the original paper that parents cause their children's autism. He ended his article by stating that autism is an innate disturbance, hence biological, and not a psychological reaction to suboptimal circumstances. It was only later, in the book *The Empty Fortress* (1967), that the psychoanalyst Bruno Bettelheim (1903–1990) made a causal link between autism and distant parents, more specifically mothers.[12] However, eventually Kanner did come to believe, under the influence of psychoanalytic explanations of autism, that there could be psychological as well as biological causes of autism.[13]

Asperger's Autism: A Lifelong Characteristic

Simultaneously, on the other side of the world, the paediatrician Hans Asperger described a similar pediatric phenomenon in his dissertation 'Die "Autistischen Psychopathen" im Kindesalter'.[14] In this text, written to obtain the degree of *Habilitation*, a postdoctoral German academic degree, Asperger described in four extensive case studies his ten-year-long observations of children in Vienna's pediatric hospital. Comparable to Kanner's statements, he offered an image of these children as being withdrawn and set apart from others: 'The autistic is only "himself" (hence the word auto), not a lively part of a bigger organism, not constantly influenced by such an organism, and constantly influencing the greater whole.'[15] Famously, Asperger describes very bright but odd children, whom he calls little professors. However, in the text itself, Asperger states that the pathology also occurs in children who are less intellectually gifted. Moreover, the level of intelligence influences how well these children

---

12 Bruno Bettelheim, *The Empty Fortress: Infantile Autism and the Birth of the Self*, illustrated edition (New York: The Free Press, 1972).

13 Brooke Ingersoll and Allison Wainer, 'The Broader Autism Phenotype', in *Handbook of Autism and Pervasive Developmental Disorders: Diagnosis, Development, and Brain Mechanisms, Volume 1, 4th Ed* (Hoboken, NJ: John Wiley & Sons Inc, 2014), pp. 28–56, https://doi.org/10.1002/9781118911389.hautc02

14 Asperger, 'Die "Autistischen Psychopathen" im Kindesalter'. Translation by the author.

15 'Der Autistische ist nur 'er Selbst' (daher das Wort auto), nicht ein lebendiger Teil eines größeren Organismus, von diesem ständig beeinflußt und ständig auf diesen wirkend.' (p. 9)

can adapt: 'Now one does not find the autistic character solely with the intellectually gifted, but also with the less gifted, yes even with the very intellectually disabled. That adaptation with the latter is much more difficult is clear.'[16] Indeed, one of the children from the text, Ernst K., seven years old, is explicitly described as cognitively disabled. For Asperger, the 'autistic psychopathy', as he calls the phenomenon, is lifelong and would also impact one's functioning lifelong. Although the condition is permanent, Asperger also thought that the unique gifts and skills that these children demonstrated also had advantages, as long as they ended up in the right place and the right circumstances. Just like Kanner, Asperger identified that the defining area in which the children struggled was their relationships with others. Through his description of the sometimes tricky and, from time to time, even cruel behaviour exhibited by some, he tells a nuanced story about their emotional lives and also recounts how the children sometimes exhibited deep emotions, such as terrible homesickness. Based on the following quote from his paper, I presume that Asperger would not agree with some present-day descriptions of autistic people which suggest that they do not have empathy:

> Given these facts, the question about the emotional lives of these children has become very complicated. We cannot merely understand it as a "poverty of emotions" from a quantitative perspective. Instead, it is a qualitatively different way of being, a disharmony of sentiment, of mental state, full of surprising contradictions by which these children are characterised and which causes their disordered adaptability.[17]

The German term 'Psychopaten' that Asperger uses sounds odd to contemporary ears and reminds us of psychopathy. However, *Autistischen Psychopathen* refers to someone with an 'autistic personality disorder'. Asperger considered autism in the first place as

---

16 'Nun findet sich der autistische Charakter keineswegs nur bei intellektuell Hochwertigen, sondern auch bei Minderbegabten, ja bei tiefstehend Schwachsinnigen. Daß in diesen letzteren Fällen eine Anpassung noch viel schwerer zu erzielen sein wird, ist klar.' (p. 31)

17 'Angesichts dieser Tatsachen ist uns das Problem der Gefühlsseite dieser Kinder sehr kompliziert geworden. Es ist jedenfalls nicht einfach nach dem Begriff „Gefühlsarmut" zu verstehen, also nach quantitativen Gesichtspunkten, es ist vielmehr ein qualitatives Anderssein, eine Disharmonie an Gefühl, an Gemüt, oft voll überraschender Widersprüche, wodurch diese Kinder charakterisiert sind, wodurch ihre Anpassungstörung verursacht wird.' (p. 56)

something innate and permanent, which is part of one's personality and identity.

The British psychiatrist Lorna Wing rediscovered the work of Asperger: she renamed the phenomenon 'Asperger syndrome' in her article from 1981, which offers a reinterpretation of the original text.[18] For Wing, Asperger syndrome is not a personality disorder but a developmental disorder. Since Wing's rediscovery, people have questioned whether Asperger syndrome is a separate entity from autistic disorder. The primary distinction would be that children with Asperger syndrome do not have a delay in language development. Wing herself proposed a spectrum of disorders with a triad of deficits: in social interaction, communication, and imagination. This triad would form the basis for later descriptions in different versions of the DSM. [19] Even today, the concepts of Kanner's autism and Asperger syndrome evoke other images, which might not meet with the complete approval of the authors of the original texts.

Autism's Past and Present

There is much more to say about the history of autism. For example, I did not elaborate on the psychogenic explanation by Bruno Bettelheim and the spread of the harmful idea of the 'refrigerator mother'. This idea primarily blamed mothers for their children's autism and resulted in the institutionalisation of many children. In response to (and reaction against) this idea, a new era dawned, ushered in by people such as Bernard Rimland (1928–2006), a psychologist with an autistic son. In this era, autism was primarily understood as being innate and neurobiological.[20] This shift in understanding autism led to decades of scientific research into the genes and neurology of autism. Rimland,

---

18   Lorna Wing, 'Asperger's Syndrome: A Clinical Account', *Psychological Medicine*, 11:1 (1981), 115–29.

19   Kathrin Hippler and Christian Klicpera, 'A Retrospective Analysis of the Clinical Case Records of "Autistic Psychopaths" Diagnosed by Hans Asperger and His Team at the University Children's Hospital, Vienna', *Philosophical Transactions of the Royal Society B: Biological Sciences*, 358:1430 (2003), 291–301, https://doi.org/10.1098/rstb.2002.1197

20   Bernard Rimland, *Infantile Autism: The Syndrome and Its Implications for a Neural Theory of Behaviour* (London: Methuen, 1964).

however, still understood autism as a rare condition, which occurs in children without intellectual disability.

The growth in diagnoses of autism over recent decades is well documented. Many explanations have been given for this, some more plausible than others. Some people argue that the expansion is due to the broadening of diagnostic criteria. Some say that there has been a diagnostic substitution of intellectual disability with autism because people consider the latter to be a less "severe" diagnosis and because there are treatments for autism that are not available for intellectual disability. Some point to environmental pollution, whereas others suggest that our society is very autismogenic: today, there is much more stress on autonomous and social functioning and far less tolerance for those who do not fit in easily. Sebastian Lundström and colleagues have suggested that it is not a question of the greater prevalence of autism traits but of diagnoses of autism.[21] The reason why such a diagnosis has become more commonplace can be attributed to the fact that doctors are more familiar with the characteristics of autism. However, another explanation may be that society has changed: flexibility and social communication is valued more, which means that people with characteristics of autism stand out more often and experience challenges in their daily functioning. [22]

For those wanting to understand autism as a phenomenon, it is essential to read the original texts by Kanner and Asperger. A crucial difference between Kanner and Asperger lies in their perspective on the nature of the condition, not the kind of people they described. Kanner suggested in his first text that infantile autism was innate, but whether it was also lifelong was less clear. He described, from a developmental perspective, how these children gradually acquired more social skills. Although, in his follow-up study, Kanner described the adults as unusual, many of them succeeded in finishing their education and established a place in society. Perhaps Kanner considered these adults

---

21   Sebastian Lundström and others, 'Autism Phenotype versus Registered Diagnosis in Swedish Children: Prevalence Trends over 10 Years in General Population Samples', *BMJ* (*Clinical Research Ed.*), 350 (2015), h1961.

22   Taskforce Autisme, 'Naar Een Autismevriendelijk Vlaanderen. Aanbevelingen van de Taskforce Autisme in Opdracht van Minister Jo Vandeurzen', 2016.

as autistic still. Nevertheless, as a child psychiatrist, he viewed autism primarily as a disorder of development.

However, for Asperger, autistic characteristics were lifelong characteristics of one's personality. Both conceptions are still relevant: autism as a developmental condition, of which the course is not fixed, and autism as an innate neurological "difference" with strengths and weaknesses. Of relevance, also, is autism's origins as firmly associated with the birth of child psychiatry. A diagnosis of autism is, therefore, also a diagnosis of a child psychiatric disorder. But what is a psychiatric diagnosis, and what is its relation with neurological development and with biology more generally? The next chapter will delve deeper into these questions.

2. The Nature of Psychiatric Diagnoses

In 2016, I attended a two-day conference for researchers of autism in Gent, Belgium. This conference was explicitly geared at autism researchers in the biomedical field. One of the speakers showed videos of a fruit fly and mouse that were supposed to exhibit autistic traits. In both animals, the researchers had changed or switched on or off a candidate gene for autism. The fruit fly exhibited autiform behaviour, so they said, i.e., behaviour that is similar to autistic behaviour, because when the researcher put the male fly in a petri dish with a female fly, he kept to himself rather than exhibiting "normal" excessive courting behaviour. Whereas the mouse exhibited extreme digging behaviour: she preferred spending her time digging holes and hiding marbles. I was intrigued about the underlying assumptions of this study: first, that these animals" behaviour is the direct result of genes. These studies suggest that a genetic explanation is a sufficient explanation for a complex phenomenon such as behaviour. However, in my opinion, behaviour is also a reaction to specific circumstances. Indeed, mice and even fruit flies have reasons for what they do, beyond merely a difference in genetic makeup. Secondly, we may wonder why we call such behaviour autistic: why do we assume that the behaviour of the mouse or the fruit fly is the same as that of autistic children? After all, we do not understand the motivations of these animals, and we may even wonder whether we properly understand the motivations of autistic children for their behaviour.

In what follows, I shall dig deeper into the question of the relationship between our mind and our body, between what is considered biological and psychological. Indeed, the relationship between psychiatric

https://doi.org/10.11647/OBP.0261.02

diagnoses and underlying biological essences such as our brains and our genes has been the subject of fierce debate. Let us set aside the nature of autism for the moment and look at how scholars have talked about mental phenomena in general. When we talk about psychiatry, we talk about the clinical discipline with the most family resemblance to philosophy. Psychiatry is not neurology: we do not merely speak about brain diseases but also about mental processes, thoughts and their meaning. Nevertheless, it is not easy to distinguish a cognitive function from a physical process in the brain. We may even wonder whether it makes sense to make this distinction. Some commentators suggest that we are simply our brains[1] and that our mental processes are mere illusions. Along the same lines, they argue that psychiatry will eventually turn out to be neurology. Surely, this cannot be the whole truth. We think about ourselves as having a mind and a self. Things have meaning for us. In mental disorders, it seems our mind has become disordered, not merely our biology.

Minds and Brains

If we want to discuss psychiatric diagnoses, we have to briefly discuss the relation between body and mind. It is not my intention here to provide a complete account of the philosophy of mind. However, a brief sketch of the discussion is necessary, as it sheds light on why our biological conceptions of autism exist. Autism seems to sit uncomfortably between the fields of psychiatry and neurology. The question 'are we our brain' has probably occupied human thoughts since the beginning of human self-consciousness. People have always asked how the mental and the corporeal relate. We have asked ourselves whether cognitive processes are merely the results of what happens in our neurons or whether, on the contrary, mental processes can also influence our brains. By the time of the ancient Greeks, people already knew that brain disorders also affect our mental processes, as is demonstrated by a quote from the *The Holy Disease*, attributed to Hippocrates: 'And men ought to know that from nothing else but (*from the brain*) come joys, delights, laughter and sports,

---

1   Dick Swaab, *Wij zijn ons brein: van baarmoeder tot Alzheimer* (London: Atlas Contact, 2010).

and sorrows, griefs, despondency, and lamentations.'[2] The holy disease is epilepsy, and according to Hippocrates, there is nothing sacred about it at all. The delusions that are associated with this disease are the result of biological processes as well. However, the fact that Hippocrates deemed it necessary to point this out to his fellow Greeks already demonstrates that viewing oneself and one's mental processes as functions of the brain was not self-evident even then. Phenomenologically speaking, we are also cognitive functions, despite all neurological images and genetic findings. I shall later argue that the solution to this conundrum does not lie in reducing experiences to biological processes. We will have to concede that many present-day views on biology are too reductionist.

The idea that there is a distinction between body and mind was stressed by René Descartes (1596–1650) in his famous distinction between *res cogitans* (mind) and *res extensa* (matter).[3] This distinction brings about a couple of conceptual problems. If *res cogitans* and *res extensa* are genuinely different things, how can they interact? The philosopher Gilbert Ryle (1900–1976) mockingly called the idea of a separate mind the ghost in the machine.[4] There are different variants to dualist thinking: one can see mind and body as separate substances and also as the same substance with distinct characteristics. The question of how such separate substances can interact occupies philosophers of consciousness even today. Some take up a radically different perspective and argue that all is matter. To some extent, I agree with the viewpoint that we are our body, and that even mental processes are matter. However, as I will argue in this book, this does not mean we can reduce mental processes to their underlying biological processes.

The challenge seems not to lie in materialism itself but in a reductionist or deterministic conception of what this materialism entails. People with a psychiatric diagnosis may display atypical behaviour. Therefore, it is often implied that dysfunctioning brains and neurons direct this behaviour entirely and in a linear fashion. We only have to look at animal models of autism, such as the mouse obsessively digging holes or the male fruit fly that is not interested in female fruit flies, to see an

---

2   Hippocrates, *De Morbo Sacro*, Section 1, http://www.perseus.tufts.edu/hopper/text?doc=Perseus%3atext%3a1999.01.0248%3atext%3dMorb.+Sacr

3   René Descartes, *Discours de la méthode* (Quebec: Collection Résurgences, 1995).

4   Gilbert Ryle, *The Concept of Mind* (Chicago: University of Chicago Press, 1949).

illustration of this. We do not know why these animals behaved as they did and to extrapolate from the behaviour of one animal to that of another (in this case, autistic humans) seems premature. I will come back later to the caveats of genetic research. However, materialist explanations of behaviour do not necessarily have to be causal-deterministic. For example, the physician Roger Penrose, a self-declared materialist, has a theory about our consciousness that builds on quantum physics and explains consciousness based on quantum processes.[5] Chapter nine will introduce new materialism, a line of thought that also allows for a non-deterministic view on the matter. Nevertheless, for many, materialism and determinism seem to be concepts that are inextricably linked.

Views on the nature of psychiatric disorders and mental processes are also relevant to our discussion about the ethics of autism and psychiatric diagnosis in general. A mere materialistic-deterministic approach seems to suggest that, in order to understand our experiences and behaviours, we should first look for causal explanations in our brains and our blueprint — our genes. However, this neglects our phenomenological experience that we are more than our neurons. It is almost impossible to imagine ourselves as something different than an 'I'. Is this 'I' merely an illusion? Moreover, such a deterministic-materialistic approach also seems to suggest that free will is an illusion. How can we indeed be free if what we want is merely a function of our brains? This question is hugely relevant to the ethics of psychiatry. It seems to be the case that most psychiatrists, and most human beings in general, do not assume a reductionist and materialistic conception about mind and body but make a distinction between the different psychiatric diagnoses. Woo-kyoung Ahn and colleagues have discovered that clinical professionals also make such a distinction.[6] In their studies, their respondents seem to consider autism as a 'very biological condition'. Moreover, the more people believe that a condition is anchored in biology, the more they deem those with the condition not to be responsible for their behaviour. Marc Miresco and Laurence Kirmayer write, in response to a survey

---

5   Roger Penrose, Abner Shimony, Nancy Cartwright, and Stephen Hawking, *The Large, the Small and the Human Mind* (Cambridge: Cambridge University Press, 2000).

6   Woo-kyoung Ahn, Caroline C. Proctor, and Elizabeth H. Flanagan, 'Mental Health Clinicians' Beliefs About the Biological, Psychological, and Environmental Bases of Mental Disorders', *Cognitive Science*, 33:2 (2009), 147–82, https://doi.org/10.1111/j.1551-6709.2009.01008.x

they conducted with 270 psychiatrists and psychologists, that the more respondents considered a specific behaviour 'psychological', the more a person was deemed responsible for it:

> The more a behavioural problem is seen as originating in "psychological" processes, the more a patient tends to be viewed as responsible and blameworthy for his or her symptoms; conversely, the more behaviours are attributed to neurobiological causes, the less likely patients are to be viewed as responsible and blameworthy.[7]

Philosopher of science Ian Hacking wrote in this respect that 'biology is exculpating'.[8]

In our interview study with adults with a recent diagnosis of autism, we also found such mechanisms.[9] Some of our female participants had already received a Borderline Personality Disorder (BPD) diagnosis before receiving their autism diagnosis. They accepted the latter diagnosis more readily. They had the impression that when clinicians still considered them to have 'borderline', unreasonable demands were made of them. For example, they had to take part in group therapy which did not work for them. As people consider autism to involve a 'different kind of brain', there was more consideration given to these women's behaviour, and they were less expected to adapt. I could not find any studies that would prove that BPD is more of a mental disorder than autism, although there is more research into the genetic basis of autism. It is difficult to grasp what it would mean for a condition to be more mental or biological. So although these distinctions are readily made and do normative work, their fundamental ontological basis may be flawed.

Biological conceptions about psychiatric disorders also have disadvantages for those diagnosed. Matthew Lebowitz and Woo-kyoung Ahn describe how biological explanations can have an impact on a clinician's empathy. If one considers a disorder to have a physical cause, people diagnosed with it are seen as less responsible for their

---

7   Marc J. Miresco and Laurence J. Kirmayer, 'The Persistence of Mind-Brain Dualism in Psychiatric Reasoning about Clinical Scenarios', *The American Journal of Psychiatry*, 163:5 (2006), 913–18, https://doi.org/10.1176/ajp.2006.163.5.913

8   Ian Hacking, *Historical Ontology* (Cambridge, MA: Harvard University Press, 2004).

9   Kristien Hens, and Raymond Langenberg, *Experiences of Adults Following an Autism Diagnosis* (Chambersburg: Palgrave Macmillan, 2018).

behaviour. However, they can also count on less empathy being shown towards them. Lebowitz and Ahn suspect that this is because people with a mental disorder that is seen as very 'biological' are considered categorically different from so-called 'normal people'. People with such diagnoses are then looked at more as mechanisms than as individual patients. Moreover, such assumptions also lead to pessimism about the prognosis: it is assumed that 'biologically based' diagnoses are less dynamic and changeable than psychological ones.[10]

The Nature of Psychiatric Disorders

What, in fact, are psychiatric disorders? As we have described above, whether people think something has a biological (rather than psychological) cause is not a sufficient criterion to demarcate psychiatric disorders from somatic illnesses. Dementia, for example, is described in DSM-5, and we assume that this is first and foremost a neurological condition. Let us accept that a psychiatric disorder is something that is described in a diagnostic handbook such as DSM-5. To know which diagnosis suits a specific person, one can use the guide's descriptions and consider to what extent we can apply these to the person who exhibits certain behaviours or who experiences specific challenges. The descriptions in the diagnostic manuals are not directly the result of or the report of scientific findings and are susceptible to changes and societal evolutions.[11] Let us, for a moment, look at the description of autism across the decades. We then see, for example, that only the DSM-5, the latest version of the DSM, mentions the idea of 'hyper or hyporeactivity to sensory input or unusual interest in sensory aspects of the environment' as a diagnostic criterion. However, since Kanner, it is considered a part of the autistic phenotype. This late addition presumably has to do with the growing voices of autistic people themselves in autistic research, who think this to be an essential aspect of their experiences. Whether the diagnostic manual describes a disorder has significant consequences.

---

10   Matthew S. Lebowitz and Woo-kyoung Ahn, 'Effects of Biological Explanations for Mental Disorders on Clinicians' Empathy', *Proceedings of the National Academy of Sciences of the United States of America*, 111:50 (2014), 17786–90, https://doi.org/10.1073/pnas.1414058111

11   Trudy Dehue, *De depressie-epidemie: over de plicht het lot in eigen hand te nemen* (Amsterdam: Atlas Contact, Uitgeverij, 2015); Trudy Dehue, *Betere mensen: over gezondheid als keuze en koopwaar* (Amsterdam: Atlas Contact, Uitgeverij, 2014).

For example, an official diagnosis is often needed to receive adequate help and support.

The reasons why a specific manual mentions certain disorders and does not mention others are not always easy to explain. Nevertheless, psychiatric diagnoses and their description become more than a mere report or a guideline for clinical action. In principle, in the DSM or other manuals, diagnoses describe clusters of behaviours and symptoms that often co-occur. Therefore, they are usually reliable, which means that different diagnosticians tend to agree on a diagnosis in an individual, but they are not necessarily valid.[12] This means that there is no guarantee that another diagnosed person's' behaviour has the same underlying explanation. However, as these clusters often co-occur, it is suspected that they could potentially represent a 'true' underlying essential disorder and be valid.

Nonetheless, for most disorders in DSM, there is no hard proof that this is the case. Besides this clustering of symptoms, a diagnostician's experience with a treatment, and the treatment's effectiveness play a role. For example, despite lobbying by stakeholders, Sensory Processing Disorder (SPD) was not retained as a separate diagnosis because the American Psychiatric Association (APA) that publishes the DSM was not convinced that this diagnosis could be a guideline for efficient therapy. Many of the children who would qualify for the proposed SPD will now either not get a diagnosis or be diagnosed with ASD or ADHD (Attention Deficit Hyperactivity Disorder) and follow these diagnoses' treatment plans. Diagnostic classification is first and foremost a clinical classification. Although scientific findings related to genetics and neurology will contribute to the categorisation of psychiatric disorders, the DSM's authors do not claim that these categories correspond to underlying biologically delineated entities. They do not claim 'to carve nature at its joints.'[13]

Still, this cannot be the entire story. We may agree that psychiatric classifications and the diagnoses based on these classifications do not

---

12   Olivier Lemeire, 'Soortgelijke stoornissen. Over nut en validiteit van classificatie in de psychiatrie', *Tijdschrift voor Filosofie*, 76:2 (2014), 217–46, https://doi.org/10.2143/TVF.76.2.3030628

13   Tijdschrift Voor Psychiatrie, *Diagnostic and Statistical Manual of Mental Disorders (5de Druk)*, Vol. 5 (2013), http://www.tijdschriftvoorpsychiatrie.nl/en/issues/472/articles/10181

necessarily correspond one-on-one to underlying biological or natural kinds. Suppose we only look at the many studies that search for the biological causes of exactly these psychiatric classifications. We then realise that they are often interpreted as referring to a fundamental underlying cause. For example, in the search for autism genes, participants are often selected based on diagnostic criteria. We might wonder why we want to use something that has a clinical finality as a basis for research into causes. How can we explain this *Verdinglichung* (reification)? Why do we conceive of human kinds (the diagnostic classifications described in the DSM) as natural kinds (biological kinds with fixed characteristics)?

Pieter Adriaens and Andreas De Block suggest some explanations in their paper 'Why we essentialise mental disorders'.[14] People could be, by nature, prone to essentialism. Moreover, the fact that specific medication, such as Ritalin, is helpful to treat someone with a specific psychiatric diagnosis, such as ADHD, suggests that it is indeed a brain disease that can be cured by medication. Trudy Dehue, in her book *Betere Mensen*, also analyses why we tend to essentialise psychiatric diagnoses: we as humans have the urge to consider something that has a name to exist in itself.[15] Psychiatric conditions that are considered real tend to work in a deculpabilising manner: they suggest that neither the person diagnosed nor their parents or immediate environment are to blame for the behaviour. However, this essentialising tendency also often leads to the fact that challenges become disorders, something inside an individual. Moreover, the description of the behaviour then transforms into the explanation of the behaviour. If a child is diagnosed with ADHD, this is based on the fact that she has problems concentrating and exhibits hyperactivity. However, ADHD will also function as the explanation for the behaviour ('she cannot sit still because she has ADHD'). By such shortcuts, one risks ignoring the contexts of and reasons for specific behaviour.

People often interpret discussions about the reality of psychiatric disorders as a denial of the reality and the impact of the suffering

---

14   Pieter R. Adriaens and Andreas De Block, 'Why We Essentialize Mental Disorders', *The Journal of Medicine and Philosophy*, 38:2 (2013), 107–27, https://doi.org/10.1093/jmp/jht008

15   Dehue, *Betere Mensen*.

experienced by the person diagnosed. Many autistic persons object to the idea that autism is not 'real'. They reject social constructivist conceptions of autism. I will discuss this in more depth in chapter four. However, it must be possible to think beyond the dichotomy of biological disease versus construct-in-language, or natural kind versus humankind. Psychiatrists, parents, children, and adults with a diagnosis testify to the realness of their experiences with autism. We do not need a fixed and straightforward biological truth to acknowledge the reality of experiences. The fact that cultural and familial contexts strongly influence specific experiences, that in a particular era of history a concept of autism may not have been applicable, and that it may not exist or be used in the future, does not take away from this. It is possible to maintain autism as a real and shared experience while at the same time acknowledging that there will probably never be a simple biological explanation. I will return to this possibility later.

Concepts of Disease

Why does some behaviour qualify for a psychiatric diagnosis? What does it mean to say that something deviates from the norm? Here we can also distinguish between naturalistic assumptions and constructionist ones. The ideas of philosopher Christopher Boorse have found much resonance in applied ethics. For Boorse, illness is deviance from the statistical mean.[16] He believes that we can draw a definite line between disease and health, and that this line is not merely the result of a value judgement. He has laid down the concept of species-typical functioning: a level of functioning that a typical member of a species would exhibit. This species-typical functioning is defined in relation to reference classes based on age and sex. We find this idea in psychiatry as well: diagnoses are often given after extensive examinations, including psychological tests. One can assess whether someone is psychologically deviant from the mean concerning social behaviour or concentration.

There are some problems associated with this approach. We can find examples where deviation from a statistical norm is not an illness, such

---

16   Christopher Boorse, 'Health as a Theoretical Concept', *Philosophy of Science*, 44:4 (1977), 542–73, https://doi.org/10.1086/288768

as height or intelligence, a fact that Boorse acknowledges. Moreover, it is not clear what it means to function in a species-typical way. Think about social behaviour: in Western societies, eye contact is seen as normal social behaviour, whereas in some other cultures, it is seen as impolite. Still, having 'appropriate' eye contact is part of the diagnostic assessment for autism. Moreover, we may wonder whether a completely value-free concept of disease is possible. Boorse has argued that homosexuality is a disease based on his idea of species-typical functioning. As he considers 'disease' as a value-free concept, this does not imply that it is either something terrible or that we should try to cure it. However, most would intuitively feel that 'homosexuality is a disease' conveys a normative claim and one we should reject.

Psychiatrist Jerome Wakefield takes a naturalistic approach, and he also makes the distinction between mental illness and health by deploying the idea of harmful dysfunction. He explicitly links disease with evolution, but allows value judgements to be part of the analysis through the use of the word 'harmful'. Something is a dysfunction if there is a defect in an internal mechanism that prevents the proper execution of a biological function.[17] A fear of spiders, for example, can be explained using the concept of evolution, but it becomes a disorder if it results in a paralysing phobia that severely hampers everyday functioning. The idea of dysfunction is also part of the present-day definition of autism. To receive a clinical diagnosis of autism, one should not merely exhibit specific behavioural characteristics, but, as I have discussed in the prologue, there should also be sufficient impact on the quality of life. We might ask ourselves whether we can ever explain this impact in evolutionary terms. Even today, many psychiatric disorders do not have clear-cut evolutionary explanations.

Furthermore, even the idea of dysfunctioning is not clear. Who gets to decide whether someone is dysfunctioning? Does dysfunctioning involve specific behaviour that is a nuisance to others? Does a child experience challenges if a particular educational system is not a good fit for her? The diagnosis of autism is often given during childhood by child psychiatrists, and this makes it even more challenging to decide whether a particular behaviour can be considered dysfunctional. In this

---

17 Jerome C. Wakefield, 'The Concept of Mental Disorder: Diagnostic Implications of the Harmful Dysfunction Analysis', *World Psychiatry*, 6:3 (2007), 149–56.

context, Courtenay Norbury and Alison Sparks state that 'the point at which normal variation converges on disorder is largely an arbitrary decision and is highly likely to be influenced by cultural values and expectations.' They note that the vast majority of therapists in Western society are white and female. However, the children with whom they work have a very diverse background concerning language and cultural experiences. For some of these children, playing with dolls is not self-evident, for example. Autism research has primarily focussed on Western culture and reflects only a small minority of the world's population.[18] In this respect, the search for evolutionary explanations or statistical means may be a lost cause from the start. Perhaps we should accept that psychiatry will never be neurology, and that value judgments will always play a role in diagnostics.

The Values of Psychiatry

The idea that psychiatry is not value-neutral has been elaborated extensively in the writings of Michel Foucault. I do not aim to discuss his arguments in much depth here, but I think it is still helpful to describe some of them. In his *Madness and Civilization: A History of Insanity in the Age of Reason*, Foucault explains that we cannot merely describe psychiatry's history as one of evolving insight: specific historical periods influence how people look at madness. Until the end of the eighteenth century, madness was a social and a moral problem. Only later did it become a medical problem.[19] Later on, Foucault discusses, through his description of the panopticon, the function of discipline. Discipline is not the same as oppression, as it is self-imposed, and its relations of power also create productive and valuable knowledge. In later writings, he describes how by opposing and partly assuming imposed identities, alternative forms of subjectivity and identity are possible. We can see these mechanisms at work if we look at how adults come to terms with their diagnosis of autism. Rather than being oppressed by a psychiatric

---

18   Courtenay Frazier Norbury and Alison Sparks, 'Difference or Disorder? Cultural Issues in Understanding Neurodevelopmental Disorders', *Developmental Psychology*, 49:1 (2013), 45–58, https://doi.org/10.1037/a0027446

19   Michel Foucault, *Geschiedenis van de waanzin in de zeventiende en achttiende eeuw* (Amsterdam: Boom, 1982).

label, autism becomes something with which one identifies. Nevertheless, this identification is not total: autism becomes an explanation for one's functioning, but at the same time, these adults also reject an overly narrow definition of what it is. Someone can identify with autism but, at the same time, say that they are empathic and social. Autism is not only something that is solely shaped by the psychiatric profession, but it acquires a life of its own as an identity.

The birth of the anti-psychiatry movement in the 1960s is, to some extent, influenced by the thoughts of Foucault. However, Foucault himself had a more nuanced view of psychiatric diagnosis. The anti-psychiatry movement, with thinkers such as psychiatrists Ronald Laing and Thomas Szasz, asserts that psychiatric diseases do not exist, as they have no biological ground. It characterises psychiatry as an authoritarian system, in which the medical profession suppresses the experiences and identities of patients. People with a psychiatric condition are not ill, and psychiatry only exists to maintain existing conceptions of normality. Hence, according to this view, psychiatry is, by definition, oppression. An oft-cited example is that of drapetomania, a presumed mental illness described in the nineteenth century by the physician Samuel Cartwright (1793–1863): drapetomania is the urge of slaves to run away from their masters. The nineteenth-century concept of hysteria might also be an example of the pathologising of justified frustrations of women in a society that suppresses them. Nowadays, the anti-psychiatry movement has been relegated to the background. Some people even use 'anti-psychiatry' as an insult aimed at those in psychiatry who advocate for change within the discipline. Nevertheless, it has led to the insight that psychiatric patients can also actively contribute to their care, rather than the psychiatrist having sole input into their treatment. Moreover, even today, there are psychiatrists and other medical professionals who question the validity of diagnoses. For example, some argue that ADHD is not a real disorder but a means to discipline normal but boisterous children with drugs. Furthermore, in the autism world, some voices want to do away with the label autism altogether. I will return to this in chapter four.

The problem with anti-psychiatry approaches is that they start from the same naive assumption as mere reductionist-biological approaches, namely that discoverable biological essences should support psychiatric classifications to be real. This idea, however, neglects how diagnoses work, and it also denies the fact that shared experiences can also have a claim to the truth. Moreover, we could ask ourselves why we would need a theory about psychiatric disorders or diagnoses. Maybe it is possible to take a pragmatic approach and claim that illness is that what brings people to the medical doctor or the psychiatrist. We could simply say that illness or disorder is that which makes people suffer. Along the same lines, perhaps we can see psychiatric classifications as a clustering of phenomena that we know how to treat. Although I have some sympathy for this pragmatic approach, it is probably insufficient. We need a theory about psychiatric classifications to serve as a legitimisation for treatment plans or medication. For a psychiatric diagnosis to work, people need to experience it as real. A pragmatic solution could then be that psychiatrists and child psychiatrists pretend to their clients that scientists know a lot about the neurological and genetic underpinnings of autism: for many people, the idea of a biological essence or cause is therapeutic. However, given the lack of knowledge about its causes and the physical and social complexity of autism, this seems a dangerous route. We will have to find an approach that does not fall into the trap of a naive-deterministic model or a naive-constructionist model, and which, at the same time, acknowledges the multi-layeredness of the meanings and experiences of psychiatric disorders.

However, first, we shall investigate how mental disorders differ from somatic disorders.

Nomy Arpaly and the Nature of Mental Illness

In her paper 'How It Is Not Just Like Diabetes', Nomy Arpaly describes how today, mental disorders are considered more and more to be like somatic diseases.[20] According to this view, a mental disorder is fundamentally different from other human conditions, such as love, fear, and hate. We do not consider the latter as diseases. Arpaly thinks this is not correct. She concedes that there are analogies between mental disorders and somatic disorders such as diabetes. For example,

---

20 Nomy Arpaly, 'How It Is Not "Just Like Diabetes": Mental Disorders and the Moral Psychologist', *Philosophical Issues*, 15:1 (2005), 282–98, https://doi.org/10.1111/j.1533-6077.2005.00067.x

medication often works very well in treating mental conditions such as depression. Moreover, you cannot decide with willpower alone not to be depressed anymore, just as this is not possible with diabetes.

Nevertheless, the most common reason people think that mental illnesses are equivalent to somatic illnesses is that people assume that mental illnesses are also located in the body. Mental illnesses are disorders of the brain, just as the body causes diabetes by being incapable of producing insulin. However, Arpaly argues, if we assumed such a materialist approach to specific mental disorders, this would apply equally to things like love and hate. If mental illnesses are brain diseases, we can also reduce love and hate to brain functionality. Although Arpaly does not deny that mental illnesses and other mental states are probably located in our biology, she still sees a difference between mental states and other biochemical conditions such as diabetes. To begin with, you can say about mental conditions that they are justified or not. For example, you can believe that a specific piece of fruit is an apple, and that can be justified or not. We can say something about whether someone's feelings of guilt are justified or unjustified. We cannot say that about purely biochemical states such as diabetes: they just 'are'. Mental states are also about something; they have content efficacy. Arpaly explains this very well using an analogy with coffee:

> Consider becoming anxious because of having had too much caffeine vs becoming anxious because there is talk of downsizing in one's company. The first case is "just like diabetes" in a way that the second case is not. This cannot be, as psychiatrists sometimes say, because the caffeine-anxiety is "biological" and the downsizing-anxiety is "not biological". Humans are biological entities, anxiety is in the brain, so presumably all anxiety is biological. However, there is still a strong difference: when the thought "I may lose my job" causes anxiety, the content or the meaning of the thought "I may lose my job" is causally efficacious in the creation of the anxiety. Unlike the thought "I may lose my job", caffeine has no content, it is not about anything, and so when it causes anxiety, it is causation that involves no content efficacy.[21]

This quote is also relevant in the context of autism. It makes clear why the distinction biological/not biological does not adequately elucidate the differences between mental and somatic disorders if we assume

---

21   Arpaly, 'How It Is Not "Just Like Diabetes"', p. 286.

that what we consider mental is biologically anchored. In the context of autism, it is presumed by some that because it is biological, it is also really almost a somatic disease that we should prevent or cure, and that explaining autism by referring to genetics or neurology is sufficient. Nevertheless, it makes sense to say that autistic behaviour also has content and is about something. It is not merely the result of an infection or mutated genes but a meaningful reaction to context. That does not mean that genes or neurology could not partly explain why people exhibit a particular behaviour, just as with bipolar disorder, for example. However, the behaviour itself is not the direct result of a flaw in genes or brains.

To illustrate her point, Arpaly uses the distinction between narcissistic personality disorder and Tourette Syndrome (TS). A narcissist who behaves arrogantly and feels superior does this because he is in fact arrogant and genuinely feels superior. In the case of TS behaviours (tics, involuntary expressions), these are the direct result of failing biology without content efficacy: TS symptoms do not indicate that a person with TS has a desire to insult you or is ill-mannered. However, in my opinion we do not know enough about people's experiences with TS to make an absolute distinction in this way.. A child psychiatrist once told me about a client with a diagnosis of TS. She was Jewish and had a specific tic, the urge to say 'Hitler', which she could suppress only with great difficulty among individual family members. Although we cannot blame her for the tics, of course, it is clear that the tics do have some mental content. We probably do not know enough about the relation between soma and psyche to say, based on diagnosis, something about the extent to which someone's thoughts, experiences, and intentions interact with one's biology. Maybe it is even the case that somatic disorders, to some extent, are *about* something and also have mental content. I shall not elaborate on this thought further here, however.

Arpaly ends the paper by explaining why many people would like mental disorders to be like diabetes. The suggestion that a mental disorder is really like a somatic disorder implies that the suffering caused by the disturbance is real:

> I think being told that one's mental troubles are like diabetes satisfies a simple, at times desperate, need: the need to have it recognised that one's

problem is real, as painful and debilitating as diabetes can be, and as unlikely to be wished away.[22]

Nevertheless, she also writes:

> Often, one has to pay dearly for the recognition that one's suffering is real. For being taken seriously in one way (being acknowledged as a real sufferer) one risks paying with giving up the privilege of being taken seriously in another way, to be taken as someone whose mental states can be meaningful and warranted. I am not referring here to the often-described experience of stigma, of being regarded as a 'lunatic', but to a type of slight, or dehumanisation, that one can encounter from the most 'enlightened' people, and which is aggravated rather than alleviated by the medical model.[23]

This is also true for autism. In my research, I have noticed that people who receive a diagnosis of autism often see this as acknowledging that their problems are real, not imaginary. The recognition of one's suffering is often inherently linked to the medicalisation of suffering precisely because the recognition is dependent on the fact that a mental disorder is considered to be biologically real. This idea is supported by the empirical studies I mentioned earlier, which shows that people diagnosed with something that is considered genetic and biological are considered to be less responsible for their deeds than people with a personality disorder.[24] Moreover, the more clinicians consider a disorder to be biological, the more often they consider medication to be the best option.[25] One study suggests, surprisingly, that clinicians and other professionals may feel less empathy towards those with a diagnosis they

---

22   Ibid., p. 295.
23   Ibid., pp. 296–7.
24   Stephen Buetow and Glyn Elwyn, 'Are Patients Morally Responsible for Their Errors?', *Journal of Medical Ethics*, 32:5 (2006), 260–62, https://doi.org/10.1136/jme.2005.012245; Marc J. Miresco and Laurence J. Kirmayer, 'The Persistence of Mind-Brain Dualism in Psychiatric Reasoning about Clinical Scenarios', *The American Journal of Psychiatry*, 163:5 (2006), 913–18, https://doi.org/10.1176/ajp.2006.163.5.913; Daniel Navon and Gil Eyal, 'Looping Genomes: Diagnostic Change and the Genetic Makeup of the Autism Population', *AJS; American Journal of Sociology*, 121:5 (2016), 1416–71, https://doi.org/10.1086/684201
25   Woo-kyoung Ahn, Caroline C. Proctor, and Elizabeth H. Flanagan, 'Mental Health Clinicians' Beliefs About the Biological, Psychological, and Environmental Bases of Mental Disorders', *Cognitive Science*, 33:2 (2009), 147–82, https://doi.org/10.1111/j.1551-6709.2009.01008.x

consider biological rather than psychological.[26] According to Arpaly, the trade-off mentioned above is unfortunate: it looks like mental disorders have to be considered as somatically 'real', like diabetes, before the suffering of people with mental conditions is taken seriously. Psychiatric diagnoses, therefore, become a kind of compensation for lack of moral imagination. People seem to have difficulties believing someone if they speak about their psychic suffering unless a diagnosis officially determines this suffering.

Nevertheless, we risk losing an opportunity to understand this suffering better. I think this is also the case with autism. The diagnosis of autism and the accompanying connotations of it being a neurological (and hence quasi-somatic) condition makes the challenges of the autistic person real, for themselves and for others. It is a confirmation that their 'being different' is not imaginary. However, reducing one's own 'being different' to a condition 'like diabetes' increases the risk that mental content, and the person's experiences, are considered less relevant.

To conclude, let us look at different models of psychiatric practice. It is interesting to examine them in light of the distinction between *Erklären* and *Verstehen*, as the philosopher Wilhelm Dilthey (1833–1911) described it.[27] *Erklären* (explaining) means looking for causal explanations, as practised by the pure sciences. *Verstehen* (understanding) gives us access to the greater whole: it allows us to understand another person and the context in which they live and function in a network of meaning of which we are also part. Verstehen, according to Dilthey, is practised in the humanities.

The differences between a psychoanalytical approach and a neurobiological approach in psychiatry are well known. Psychoanalysis stresses the importance of language, of the subconscious and early experiences from childhood. Psychoanalytic therapy can take years and

---

26 Matthew S. Lebowitz and Woo-kyoung Ahn, 'Effects of Biological Explanations for Mental Disorders on Clinicians' Empathy', *Proceedings of the National Academy of Sciences of the United States of America*, 111:50 (2014), 17786–90, https://doi.org/10.1073/pnas.1414058111

27 Wilhelm Dilthey, 'Entwürfe Zur Kritik Der Historischen Vernunft Erster Teil: Erleben, Ausdruck Und Verstehen' in *Der Aufbau Der Geschichtlichen Welt in Den Geisteswissenschaften*, Volume 7 (Göttingen: Vandenhoeck & Ruprecht, 1992), pp. 191–251; Wilhelm Dilthey, 'Ideen Über Eine Beschreibende Und Zergliedernde Psychologie (1894)' in *Die Geistige Welt*, Volume 5 (Göttingen: Vandenhoeck & Ruprecht, 1990), pp. 139–240.

is often concerned with looking for insight rather than finding practical solutions and causal explanations. In some aspects, the psychoanalytical approach is usually not that different from the neurobiological approach. In some schools, finding explanations is at least as important as understanding one's functioning. Autism is an especially good example here: psychogenic explanations of autism have blamed mothers and led to the institutionalisation of children. Still, a psychoanalytic approach has the advantage that clients are considered more than their diagnoses. Such an approach searches for meaning in experiences.

Theoretically, according to a purely neurobiological approach, psychiatric conditions are assumed to be diseases in our brain. Psychiatry becomes a way to understand the world of neurons and genes. I concede that neurology is an essential aspect of understanding psychiatric illnesses. Nevertheless, such an approach may entail situating the disorder merely in the individual and may risk neglecting the context. Moreover, such a neurobiological approach would seem to suggest that medication is the best option. In Belgium, at least, many present-day psychiatrists do not work merely in a psychoanalytic way and do not consider themselves purely neuropsychological psychiatrists either. George L. Engel's bio-psycho-social model tries to think several aspects through together and states that the different mental phenomena are situated on different levels (biological, psychological, social). We have to approach these different levels in an integrated way. This approach has received some criticism as well: it is eclectic and not sustained by a solid theoretical framework.[28] I still think that in this approach, understanding is an integral part of treatment.

It is refreshing to consider the ideas of psychiatrist and philosopher Karl Jaspers (1883–1969). He opposed the psychoanalytic approach of his time because he thought that, rather than understanding patients, such a system sought to unmask them and their disorder. His phenomenological-hermeneutic practice of psychiatry championed an empathic understanding of the patient. In his work *Allgemeine Psychopathologie* (1913), he stresses the importance of being able, as a clinician, to take different perspectives, including biological perspectives, and incorporating the greater context of culture as a

---

28   S. Nassir Ghaemi, *The Rise and Fall of the Biopsychosocial Model: Reconciling Art and Science in Psychiatry* (Baltimore: JHU Press, 2010).

whole.[29] A psychiatrist must search for a comprehensive understanding of phenomena, not merely reduce them to mechanistic explanations. However, he did see a role for *explanation* in psychiatry. According to Jaspers, some mental phenomena, such as psychosis, are so strange and different that they are beyond *Verstehen*. We should explain these phenomena biologically. Jaspers' *Allgemeine Psychopathologie* is a strikingly modern read and should, in my view, be compulsory literature in training for psychiatrists. In a phenomenon such as autism, we can wonder where *Verstehen* ends, and *Erklären* begins. Autistic children and adults are still often considered to be strange and incomprehensible. Nevertheless, it may be the duty of medical professionals, and ourselves, to continue to attempt to understand behaviour that appears bizarre and incomprehensible at first. The autistic person who does not speak and does not score highly on an IQ test has a reason for his or her behaviour, which we must strive to understand.

The first meaning of autism is that it is defined as a psychiatric disorder in a diagnostic manual. In this chapter, we have investigated what a psychiatric disorder is. We investigated the relationship between mind and brain, psychology and biology. We saw how biological explanations for mental disorders can take away feelings of guilt and open up routes towards healing. However, reductionist approaches that merely give a causal biological explanation of mental disorders neglect the importance of understanding the meaning and context in which phenomena occur. To understand this better, let us investigate what kinds of explanations have been given for autism. In the next chapter, I shall describe several theories that have attempted to explain the specific behaviour associated with autism. I shall demonstrate that these theories have normative import as well. Deciding upon the theory that is presumed to underlie certain behaviour is also a moral choice.

---

29 Karl Jaspers, *General Psychopathology* (Baltimore: JHU Press, 1997).

3. Cognitive Explanations of Autism

Beyond Theory of Mind

When I first started to research issues related to autism, way back in 2011, I set out to answer traditional bioethical questions such as 'is a prenatal diagnosis for autism ethically justified?'. Almost a decade later, I consider the idea that we can even predict autism prenatally, based on genes, naive. However, back then, a logical place to start the investigation was the book *The Ethics of Autism*, written by Deborah Barnbaum.[1] As she wrote the book in 2008, we may excuse the author for taking the then prevailing explanatory model of autism, a deficit in Theory of Mind (ToM), as a starting point for ethical reflection. Less excusable is that she believes that, given this deficit, autistics are 'among us' but never truly 'of us', to paraphrase the book's subtitle. Hence the use of reproductive technologies to avoid the birth of a child with autism, she states, is permissible. The book is an illustration and a warning sign of how ontological assumptions about autism profoundly influence the ethical conclusions we draw. Assumptions about empathy and autism have tempted many moral philosophers to use autism as an example in a reflection on the nature of morality in general. The way we explain autism also has repercussions for the people diagnosed with autism. Imagine a scholar who argues that an autistic person can discern emotions neither in themselves nor in fellow human beings. Such a scholar has an entirely different starting point from someone who thinks that a person's apparently awkward social functioning results

---

1   Deborah Barnbaum, *The Ethics of Autism: Among Them, But Not of Them* (Bloomington: Indiana University Press, 2008).

    https://doi.org/10.11647/OBP.0261.03

from experiencing an overload of sensory input.[2] Therefore we must dig deeper into some of these assumptions and their consequences.

In previous chapters, we have seen how a diagnosis of autism is generally a clinical diagnosis. In consultation with other professionals, in a multidisciplinary team with psychologists and other caregivers, a psychiatrist proposes a diagnosis based on behavioural criteria from the diagnostic manual and based on assessing the person's functioning. A diagnosis is the starting point for services and support, a clinical presentation based on which clinicians can devise a suitable therapeutic trajectory. However, for many people, autism as a concept also refers to something else, a specific neurological and biological reality, a way of being, a different way of thinking, sensing or feeling. Consider the term 'neurodiversity', a name that refers explicitly to a neurologically atypical way of being. Following this, some argue that autism, because it is a neurological or genetic difference, is also a neutral difference or an identity in the same way as homosexuality. Therefore, society should support and accept autistic people rather than try to cure them.[3] However, people have also used this emphasis on the neurological basis of autism to defend further research into the genetics and neurology of autism and to look further for medical treatments.

Explanations of autism take place on different levels. For example, we can explain it by referring to genetic factors, or by neurological and cognitive functioning that causes specific behaviour. Often the influence of physical and social environments on the expression of autistic behaviour is also mentioned. Many models seek to integrate these. However, even in such integrative models, some key questions remain: what *is* autism, the behaviour or the cognitive explanation? To which extent does our genetic blueprint steer behaviours, and how can mental models explain particular challenges that autistic people face? I shall postpone discussing the genetics of autism to chapter 11, and I will now sketch the explanatory models that have appealed both to the public imagination and to philosophers and ethicists alike.

---

2   Nick Pentzell, 'I Think, Therefore I Am. I Am Verbal, Therefore I Live', in *The Philosophy of Autism*, ed. by Jami L. Anderson and Simon Cushing (Lanham: Rowman & Littlefield, 2013), pp. 103–8.

3   Pier Jaarsma and Stellan Welin, 'Autism as a Natural Human Variation: Reflections on the Claims of the Neurodiversity Movement', *Health Care Analysis*, 20.1 (2012), pp. 20–30.

Why We Need to Talk about Theory of Mind

Since Kanner and Asperger, researchers have sought to define the origins of the different behaviour of autistics as a deficit of social capabilities. The most widely known theory is that autistic people have a deficient Theory of Mind (ToM), an idea that was first used in 1978 by David Premack and Guy Woodruff. Theory of Mind refers to the capacity to draw conclusions about the mental states of others.[4] The ability to judge what others think typically develops in children around the third year of their lives. Whether a young child has a properly functioning ToM can be tested using the Sally-Anne false-belief test. The investigator shows the child a puppet show with the dolls Sally and Anne, a basket, a box, and a marble. Sally puts the marble in the basket while Anne watches. Sally goes outside, and Anne takes the marble from the basket and puts it in the box, without Sally seeing it. The test taker then asks the child where Sally will look for the marble in the basket or the box.

The expected answer is 'basket'. Most children pass this test at around age four. Children with a diagnosis of autism succeed at a later age. This finding led autistic researchers to conclude that autistic people may be unaware of the fact that other people also have thoughts and intentions. In particular, the British researcher Simon Baron-Cohen has further examined this theory and popularised it. Autistic people do not readily look others in the eyes. Eyes are, it is said, the window to the soul, and for someone who seemingly has difficulty understanding that there is a soul behind those windows, it makes no sense to look into them.[5] If one begins with the idea that autistic people have a deficient ToM, one might readily conclude that these people have no, or at least less, empathy. To have empathy, you have to be able to imagine what another person feels.

Some people have raised critiques of the ToM hypothesis itself, as well as how ToM is tested, and the idea that autistic people have an empathy deficit. Autistic people themselves claim to have empathy.

---

4   David Premack and Guy Woodruff, 'Does the Chimpanzee Have a Theory of Mind?', *Behavioural and Brain Sciences*, 4.4 (1978), 515–629.

5   Simon Baron-Cohen, Alan Leslie, and Uta Frith, 'Does the Autistic Child Have A "Theory of Mind"?', *Cognition*, 21.1 (1985), 37–46; Simon Baron-Cohen, *Mindblindness: An Essay on Autism and Theory of Mind* (Cambridge, MA: MIT Press, 1997).

According to the empathy imbalance theory, they may even feel too much, with the result that they have to close themselves off from others.[6] Autistic children can pass the Sally-Anne test by researching the correct outcome, if they have the motivation to do so. [7] A very recent theory by Eliane Deschrijver and Colin Palmer states that autistics may not have difficulty inferring mental states in others, but in discerning these from their own mental states.[8]

Moreover, some researchers claim, autism is something that develops far earlier than their third year, at an age when no child has a functioning ToM.[9] A deficit in ToM could merely be the symptom of a development that was atypical far earlier on. In this respect, Shaun Gallagher has stated that the autistic person explicitly reflects on other people's intentions far more than a typically functioning person. They have missed out on something at a more fundamental developmental level: they did not learn how to understand others instinctively in spontaneous interaction (without theory).[10] Moreover, specific research demonstrated that although autistic children might score less on ToM tests than their typically developing peers, they often acquire the skill later.[11]

Bridging Minds

Scholars with a background in disability studies and sociology have described autism as a defect that we can localize in the individual or in an individual's inability to interpret someone else's mood and behaviour'. A

6   Adam Smith, 'The Empathy Imbalance Hypothesis of Autism: A Theoretical Approach to Cognitive and Emotional Empathy in Autistic Development', *Psychological Record*, 59.2 (2009), pp. 273–94.

7   Candida C. Peterson and others, 'Children with Autism Can Track Others' Beliefs in a Competitive Game', *Developmental Science*, 16.3 (2013), 443–50, https://doi.org/10.1111/desc.12040

8   Eliane Deschrijver & Colin Palmer, 'Reframing social cognition: Relational versus representational mentalizing,' *Psychological Bulletin*, 146:11 (2020), pp 941–69.

9   R. Peter Hobson, 'Against the Theory of "Theory of Mind"', *British Journal of Developmental Psychology*, 9.1 (1991), 33–51, https://doi.org/10.1111/j.2044-835X.1991.tb00860.x

10   Shaun Gallagher, 'Understanding Interpersonal Problems in Autism: Interaction Theory As an Alternative to Theory of Mind', *Philosophy, Psychiatry, and Psychology*, 11.3 (2004), pp. 199–217.

11   Yael Kimbi (2014). Theory of mind abilities and deficits in Autism Spectrum Disorders. *Topics in Language Disorders*, 34(4), 329–43.

good example is the paper 'Minds Between Us: Autism, Mindblindness and the Uncertainty of Communication',[12] written by Anne E. McGuire and Rod Michalko. In this paper, the authors challenge the ideas that social and communicative challenges arise from an individual defect. McGuire and Michalko state that people continuously associate autism with mystery. We have to solve a medical puzzle: if we do not understand certain behaviour, we have to explain it by finding a biological origin. If we gather enough knowledge about what autism *is*, what causes it, we can know it and prevent or cure it. Behavioural therapies can then help to alleviate autistic symptoms and improve the behaviour of the autistic child. According to McGuire and Michalko, this interpretation is wrong. Autism is a complex process that takes place in interactions between people. Autism only has meaning in a relational context, and because of that, autism can teach us something about the interactions between people in general. We can never be entirely sure that what another person means with a specific message is precisely the same as how we have understood it. Communication between people is always partial.

If we consider autism a problem of communication by the individual, we assume a standard of problem-free communication in which non-autistic people can participate. This is clear in the Sally-Anne test, where we believe that the correct answer is that Sally thinks that her marble is still in the basket. This 'correct' answer means that you passed the test. If you give a different answer, then you fail. Nevertheless, this is a denial of what communication is. Readily reading someone's intentions based on the look in their eyes seems nice in theory but is not how communication works. We do not just read another's intentions; we must actively work to reconstruct and interpret them, a process that is not always without problems. To go back to the Sally-Anne test: there might be reasons why someone would think that the marble is not in the original place, reasons that do not necessarily relate to reading Sally's thoughts. For example, Sally may know Anne very well and may think that Anne could have played a joke on her. There is more at stake than purely reading the mind of someone else. Nonetheless, in the standard account of autism, part of the puzzle is deemed to be that autistic people have a deficient Theory of Mind, which we can assess using tests such as Sally-Anne.

According to the ToM theory of autism, it is a condition in which something has gone wrong in the individual's natural cause of development. McGuire and Michalko also refer to the ideas of Michael Tomasello and others, which situate what is characteristically human in the possibility of shared attention and the development of shared aims.[13] Tomasello and colleagues argue that possessing a greater or lesser number of these characteristics is proof of how 'close to nature' certain people are: primates and autistic children would, in their view, not be able to participate in activities that require shared attention. According to McGuire and Michalko, however, this assumption neglects the idea that there is a moment in all communication in which one has to make an effort to understand the other in a way that makes sense. They use the ideas of Judith Butler and Emmanuel Levinas to argue that the other is someone who breaks through our barriers and questions us. The other is the other in an absolute way: the other forces us to think about who we are and our relation to that other. We are very close to the other but also infinitely far away. The other can not merely be known or resolved. We can all only guess the true intentions of the other. In this way, autism can teach us something about ourselves and how communication always brings uncertainty.

This is one of the great merits of McGuire and Michalko's work. Besides the image of autism as a medical puzzle to be solved, it is also often associated with something completely unusual. Often, images of Martians and other aliens are used to stress this otherness, even by people who have a diagnosis themselves. An unbridgeable gap is thus created between the 'neurotypical' and the 'autistic'. If we follow McGuire and Michalko and conceive of autism as something that unavoidably takes place within communication, it allows us to understand the autistic other better. We can all imagine situations when we have understood something completely differently from how it was intended or when we did not understand a joke. This fact does not preclude the notion that autistic people suffer from such instances more frequently or intensely, but it allows us to understand each other better.

---

13   Tomasello Michael and Carpenter Malinda, 'Shared Intentionality', *Developmental Science*, 10.1 (2006), 121–25, https://doi.org/10.1111/j.1467-7687.2007.00573.x

Beyond the Theory of Mind

Simon Baron-Cohen has championed the association of autism with both a deficit in ToM and with less empathy. Baron-Cohen has sympathy for autistic persons and stresses the talents that these people often have. In his later research, he elaborates on the idea of the extreme male brain.[14] According to this theory, specific characteristics that we primarily associate with men are amplified in autism. Autistic people primarily systemise and analyse, in contrast to the more socially interested empathisers. Therefore they have more insight into details. The association of autism with some characteristics that we primarily associate with men looks straightforward: even today, three-fourths of those diagnosed with autism are male.

Moreover, Baron-Cohen gives an additional biological explanation for the origins of autism by linking it to increased exposure to testosterone in the uterus. Anyone who has read up on gender studies intuits that we can contest this theory on several grounds, not in the least the way it is named. Associating specific characteristics with being male or female seems outdated. Moreover, what about autistic girls and women? Do we say that girls in STEM or girls who prefer activities that are not necessarily related to caring have more 'male characteristics'?[15] This illustrates that scientists should take care when using specific terms. Still, Baron-Cohen is a big proponent of the idea of neurodiversity: being autistic has certain advantages. For example, it can significantly improve your performance in certain professions to be an analytic thinker and to focus primarily on details. Baron-Cohen has proposed that we should no longer speak of Autism Spectrum Disorder but Autism Spectrum Condition, to stress that we should not always consider the characteristics of autistic people a disorder.[16]

With the idea of hyper-systemizing — primarily paying attention to analysis and details rather than to interpersonal aspects — we approach

---

14 Simon Baron-Cohen, 'The Extreme Male Brain Theory of Autism', *Trends in Cognitive Sciences*, 6.6 (2002), 248–54.

15 STEM is an abbreviation of Science, Technology, Engineering & Mathematics.

16 Simon Baron-Cohen, 'Is Asperger Syndrome/High-Functioning Autism Necessarily a Disability?', *Development and Psychopathology*, null.03 (2000), 489–500, https://doi.org/null; Simon Baron-Cohen, 'Editorial Perspective: Neurodiversity — a Revolutionary Concept for Autism and Psychiatry', *Journal of Child Psychology and Psychiatry*, 58.6 (2017), 744–47, https://doi.org/10.1111/jcpp.12703

the next explanatory model of autism. For Uta Frith and others, the fundamental deficit that can explain the behaviour of autistic people is weak central coherence.[17] Central coherence is the ability to integrate different sensory and informational perceptions in a whole. For autistic people, it is a challenge to tie together all these different sensations and feelings into a sensible whole. People with autism get stuck on the details. As such, weak central coherence also explains other challenges that autistic people experience. A focus on details could make it difficult to perceive other people as whole beings with their own thoughts and selves, explaining why autistic children sometimes fail false-belief tests such as the Sally-Anne test. It would also explain why autistic people sometimes have different sensory experiences. Uta Frith and other proponents of this theory would claim that it is not the case that autistic people, for example, perceive certain sounds as louder. Because they cannot integrate them into a greater whole, they only seem louder to them. We should, therefore, take the accounts of autistic people about their sensory perceptions with a grain of salt. Here we also arrive at the most problematic part of her theory: not only do autistic people have a deficient ToM in relation to other people, but also in relation to themselves.

We can represent our self as a little man, a homunculus that is the integrated sum of our experiences. This unified self-experience is thus deficient or fragmented in autistic people. Because of this deficient 'self', we should be cautious when we interpret the experiences that autistic people tell us they have, and we should double-check these with their caregivers. I immediately want to express some concerns here. First, we can contest the idea of the self as a homunculus.[18] Philosophers of consciousness disagree about what it means to have a self. It is therefore misguided to deny certain people the ability to speak authoritatively about their own experiences based on this assumption. Moreover, empirical research seems to suggest that autistic people do have a strong sense of self and often question what it means to have a self.[19] This self

---

17   Uta Frith, *Autism: Explaining the Enigma*, 2nd ed. (Malden, MA: Blackwell Pub, 2003).

18   Markus Gabriel, *I Am Not a Brain: Philosophy of Mind for the 21st Century* (Hoboken: Wiley, 2017).

19   David Williams, 'Theory of Own Mind in Autism Evidence of a Specific Deficit in Self-Awareness?', *Autism*, 14.5 (2010), 474–94, https://doi.org/10.1177/13623613 10366314

may be less spontaneous or less subconscious than in an average person. However, we could also state that this is precisely because autistic people are excellent witnesses of their own experiences. In chapter six, I shall return to the problem of epistemic injustice and who can speak for whom.

Ideas about a deficient ToM assume that autism is a problem at a social level in the first place. Competing theories are based on this as well. For example, Peter Hobson has stated that during the early years of autistic children, even before there is any development of ToM, something atypical happens as they learn spontaneous and atheoretical social interaction. These children are, from birth, focused on others to a lesser degree than neurotypical children.[20] However, if we look at the DSM-5 definition of ASD, we notice that social-communicative problems are only one part of the dyad. Repetitive or stereotypical behaviour is the other part. More recently, theories have been developed that assume that autism is a problem with information processing or sensory processing in the first place, and that social challenges are the result of this, rather than the other way around. For a long time, it has been known that autistic people have problems with executive functioning. Cognitive science defines executive functions as those that play a role in planning, concentration, and working memory. Because autistic people have difficulties with their executive functions, they experience challenges in planning and being attentive to different things simultaneously.[21] Therefore, they have a preference for repetitive actions, which also explains the well-known insistence of sameness, an aversion to change.[22] If you are unsure of how to take the next step, it is safer if everything remains the same. Explanations that refer to executive functions have an advantage in that they are close to what autistic people tell themselves. They could also explain the overlap of autism with ADHD. Nonetheless, we can still wonder

---

20 R. Peter Hobson, 'Against the Theory of "Theory of Mind"', *British Journal of Developmental Psychology*, 9.1 (1991), 33–51, https://doi.org/10.1111/j.2044-835X.1991.tb00860.x

21 Francesco Craig and others, 'A Review of Executive Function Deficits in Autism Spectrum Disorder and Attention-Deficit/Hyperactivity Disorder', *Neuropsychiatric Disease and Treatment*, 12 (2016), 1191–202, https://doi.org/10.2147/NDT.S104620

22 James Russell, *Autism as an Executive Disorder* (Oxford: Oxford University Press, 1997).

whether a deficit in executive functioning is an explanatory model in itself, or the result of a difference on a more fundamental level of information processing.

Beyond Deficit Models of Autism

In the last decade, scholars have developed theories that explicitly take into account the experiences of autistic persons. In a 2007 paper, Henry Markram, Tania Rinaldi, and Kamila Markram describe their Intense World theory.[23] The problems and challenges that autistic people face, they claim, can be explained by sensory perceptions being experienced much more intensely. They argue that this is because local neuronal circuits in autistic people are hyperreactive and hyperplastic, something the authors have studied in mice. This theory has been much acclaimed by autistic people because it is close to what they experience as their primary challenge. For example, Nick Pentzell, who is autistic himself, writes that this overload explains why children fail the Sally-Anne test. During this test, these children are so busy attempting to maintain their equilibrium while experiencing an overflow of sensory input that everything else becomes a side issue: 'sensory overload inhibits *anyone* from thinking about much more than surviving its barrage'.[24]

Laurent Mottron is a psychiatrist working at the University of Montréal. He is originally from France and has rejected the psychoanalytic assumptions about autism that are prevalent there. His theory is called Enhanced Perceptual Functioning.[25] For Mottron, who also intensively collaborates with autistic researchers (amongst others Michelle Dawson), autism is a different form of intelligence. In his book on early detection, he stresses that autistic people can see wholes and

---

23 Henry Markram, Tania Rinaldi, and Kamila Markram, 'The Intense World Syndrome — an Alternative Hypothesis for Autism', *Frontiers in Neuroscience*, 1:1 (2007), 77–96, https://doi.org/10.3389/neuro.01.1.1.006.2007

24 Nick Pentzell, 'I Think, Therefore I Am. I Am Verbal, Therefore I Live', in *The Philosophy of Autism*, ed. by Jami L. Anderson and Simon Cushing (Lanham: Rowman & Littlefield, 2013), pp. 103–8.

25 Laurent Mottron and others, 'Enhanced Perceptual Functioning in Autism: An Update, and Eight Principles of Autistic Perception', *Journal of Autism and Developmental Disorders*, 36:1 (2006), 27–43, https://doi.org/10.1007/s10803-005-0040-7

not only details, despite what other theories may suggest.[26] They just arrive via a different route to the whole. Therefore one should not try to force an autistic child with a delayed language development to learn a language. Autistic children firstly develop a good visual intelligence, which is apparent in the fact that at a young age they can often already read letters ('hyperlexia'). Only after that do they acquire oral language. We should not try to force them to follow more typical development pathways; this might even be considered unethical.

Interestingly, Mottron makes a distinction between 'real' autism and syndromic autism. The latter is autistic behaviour that we can entirely explain by an underlying syndrome such as Fragile-X, a condition with a localizable genetic cause that is associated with autistic behaviours. Although it is possibly correct that different biological causes of autism lead to different types of autism, it seems that the distinction between autism-as-the-result-of-a-syndrome and autism-as-visual-intelligence is artificial and undesirable. Autistic people with a known syndrome behave a certain way because of specific reasons, and they can also have qualities related to their autism. For these people, it is vital that we try to understand their behaviours and not merely explain them via genes.

Moreover, and I think this is a valid criticism of all explanatory models, it seems impossible to find one explanatory model that covers all autistic behaviours. There will be people diagnosed with autism who do not experience much empathy or who score poorly on the visual parts of an IQ test. Autism as a diagnosis connects these people in a way that often makes sense, based on shared experiences. A vision of autism that tries to reduce it to one explanatory model carries the risk that some people will not fit that model, and that we therefore deny them the benefits of identifying and being identified as autistic. We can conclude, however, that we should reject a theory in which no one with a diagnosis recognizes themselves, and which is purely based on speculation about how brains work.

More recent models of autism assume the Bayesian model of predictive coding, the idea that our brain continually generates statistical models of reality and adjusts these based on new information. The High, Inflexible Precision of Prediction Errors in Autism (HIPPEA) theory by

---

26   Laurent Mottron, *L'intervention précoce pour enfants autistes: Nouveaux principes pour soutenir une autre intelligence* (Brussels: Editions Mardaga, 2016).

KU Leuven researcher Sander Van de Cruys states that autism is related to difficulties in evaluating the weight of prediction errors.[27] Our brains build a model based on our observations, and this model is adjusted based on mistakes in our prediction. However, not every prediction error is relevant: some are noise or not appropriate for a specific task. Autistic people's brains put too much weight on all mistakes and do not filter out the noise. Therefore it is more challenging to come to specific predictions, and the brain considers every new situation to be entirely new. This model allows us to view autism not merely as a deficiency. In tasks where the context could lead to mistakes in typically functioning people, for example, in visual illusions, autistic participants often score better.

The Ethical Import of Ontological Assumptions about Autism

Let us, for the moment, set aside the discussion about the explanatory models of autism and look at their relevance for ethics. A branch of ethics in which autism has flourished, for example, is that of meta-ethics. Autism has inspired some philosophers to speculate about the question of why and how we are moral beings. An example of this is the discussion between Victoria McGeer and Jeanette Kennett. In her article 'Autism, Empathy and Moral Agency', Kennett tries to tackle the age-old question about whether David Hume or Immanuel Kant is correct regarding the role of emotions in morality. Autistic people, especially those Kennett describes as 'high-functioning', have a sense of duty and justice. Kennett takes Kant's side: emotions can play a role in morality, but they do not have to. There are other ways to arrive at moral action. According to her, autistic people are Kantians par excellence. Because they do not have direct access to the intuitions and feelings of others, they come to moral insight through reasoning about what is good. She refers to Oliver Sacks and Temple Grandin's meetings, where the latter stated that she would consider for herself how people behaved and what to learn from this. Kennett concludes that, driven by the desire

---

27 Sander Van de Cruys and others, 'Precise Minds in Uncertain Worlds: Predictive Coding in Autism', *Psychological Review*, 121:4 (2014), 649–75, https://doi.org/10.1037/a0037665

to do good, autistic people use reason to arrive at what is good. Hence, she concludes that although empathy may play a practical role in moral development, it is not a precondition to be a moral actor.[28]

Victoria McGeer explains the moral actions of autistic people differently in her text, *Varieties of Moral Agency*.[29] She points out that autistic people are often prone to describe themselves and others in terms of moral duties. From autobiographies, she deduces that autistic people often have difficulties predicting others' behaviour, leading to anxiety. They, therefore, need structure and order. Their desire for just rules might be more related to their passion for a structured world rather than intrinsically moral. As McGeer points out herself, it is difficult to draw a distinction between following rules as a protective mechanism and honestly acting morally in the way Kant would have wanted. Next, McGeer states that the necessity to create order to deal with the environment contributes to the fact that autistic people are very passionate about their desire for order. Therefore it is not only reason that drives their moral action but also their strong underlying feelings about order and structure that make autistic people use rationality to arrive at this order. Rationality is the means to acquire the passionately sought-after aim: order and structure.

Furthermore, so McGeer concludes, it is precisely because autistic people have these passions that many of them develop into true moral actors. Kennett and McGeer wrote their works in 2002 and 2008. More than ten years later, we still do not agree on the core explanation of autism, and the idea that autistic people have an empathy deficit needs revision. Experiences and scientific studies demonstrate that autistic people are not by definition less empathic than others.[30] Philosophers and ethicists ought to study the experiences of many different autistic people. Perhaps as for morality, the same is true for autism: it may make more sense to study the phenomenon in its multiplicity, rather than reduce it to a single explanatory model.

---

28 Jeanette Kennett, 'Autism, Empathy and Moral Agency', *Philosophical Quarterly*, 52:208 (2002), 340–57.

29 Victoria McGeer, 'Varieties of Moral Agency: Lessons From Autism (and Psychopathy)', in *Moral Psychology, Volume 3*, ed. by Walter Sinnott-Armstrong (Cambridge, MA: MIT Press, 2008).

30 Indrajeet Patil and others, 'Divergent Roles of Autistic and Alexithymic Traits in Utilitarian Moral Judgments in Adults with Autism', *Scientific Reports*, 6 (2016), 23637, https://doi.org/10.1038/srep23637

The explanatory model of autism that one adopts effects how autism can be used to illustrate specific ideas about the role of empathy in morality. It also has consequences for how we think about the moral responsibility of autistic people themselves. Can autism be used to excuse the transgression of particular social, ethical, or legal norms? It is this question that Ken Richman and Raya Bidshahri tackle in their paper 'Autism, Theory of Mind and the Reactive Attitudes'.[31] Reactive attitudes are feelings of approval and disapproval as a response to specific deeds. As Peter Strawson (1919–2006) has argued in his seminal paper 'Freedom and Resentment',[32] they play a role in how we think about moral responsibility. Reactive attitudes are feelings of approval, disapproval, and praise as a response to specific deeds. If we think about whether an act is good or bad, we also think about the effects that this deed potentially has on ourselves and others. If we are responsible for our deeds, we will have to be able to estimate the reactive attitudes that these deeds can cause. We require a minimum of empathy for this. Richman states that there is no reason to assume that autistic people cannot participate in the moral community: they make moral judgements and give reasons for them. Members of the moral community can do things that are not right as well. We cannot, however, blame autistic people for all their transgressions. Suppose it is so that autistic people cannot properly judge reactive attitudes because they have a deficient Theory of Mind. In that case, if they perform a particular moral transgression, they are not responsible for it. Richman and Bidshahri do not claim that a deficient ToM is the correct explanation for autism, or that the idea of reactive attitudes is the proper way to look at morality. They demonstrate that, should these two approaches be correct, this could have consequences for the extent to which autistic people are responsible for their behaviour. If we cannot understand which reactions our actions will evoke in others, how are we responsible? Moreover, Richman and Bidshahri raise an important point: to what extent is it the duty of the autistic person to put more effort into trying to understand others? Should non-autistic persons demonstrate more understanding for their

---

31   Kenneth Richman and Raya Bidshahri, 'Autism, Theory of Mind, and the Reactive Attitudes', *Bioethics*, 2017.

32   Peter Frederick Strawson, 'Freedom and Resentment', *Proceedings of the British Academy*, 48 (1962), 1–25.

autistic fellow human beings, explain the context of specific reactions of theirs, and try to come to mutual understanding?

I would also argue that being responsible and being held accountable are not the same. Holding someone responsible and having reactive attitudes also imply seeing the other as a human being capable of learning. I usually give the somewhat autobiographical example of pathological clumsiness. Imagine an utterly clumsy person, to the extent that, throughout their life, they have broken many glasses of wine, spilt coffee, and ruined people's clothes to a far greater degree than is acceptable. This person regrets this profoundly but cannot help their behaviour. Does this mean that their partner has no reason at all to be grumpy, perhaps even a bit angry when they once again spill the last glass in the bottle of wine? Is a cheerful 'oh that is fine, you cannot help it' always an appropriate reaction? Grumpiness may not be related to the other person's capacity to have done otherwise, as much as it is a sign that the other is considered a completely autonomous, but, in some respects, flawed human.

Reactive attitudes also serve a pedagogical aim. Even if we know that a particular faux pas was beyond the control of a given person, complete indifference is not the proper reaction. It assumes that the person doing the transgression is beyond any learning. In my experience, autistic people want acknowledgement of the fact that they do some things because they do not understand the effects on others, and they did not intend any harm. Nevertheless, they also like to learn and receive feedback and explanations. This does not mean forcing them to conform to certain norms, but it can be part of the mutual understanding described above.

To conclude this chapter, I would like to give the floor to M. Remi Yergeau and Bryce Huebner. In an article they wrote as a dialogue, they challenge the use of ToM arguments in philosophy. They state that all ethicists and philosophers who take this approach make the same mistake: they assume that a social deficit is the basis of autism. This way of thinking has dehumanized autistic people and has directly impacted their lives. Yergeau talks about how certain philosophers use autobiographies of autistic people to demonstrate that they have a deficient emotional experience rather than as a way to gain access to this emotional life. Such philosophers hunt for symptoms to illustrate the lack of ToM. This endeavour is an example of a deficiency in Theory of the Autistic Mind that belongs to the autism researchers themselves. They do not put much effort into engaging autistic people in their research, and they do not check certain presumptions for their empirical truth. Yergeau summarizes this as follows:

> ToM is both a rhetorical and philosophical problem: it impoverishes not only our notions of what it means to have a body mind, to exist, to cogitate, or to participate, but it also reduces how we interrelate or think about interrelating. The idea of others outside oneself is both rhetorically and philosophically complicated (understatement of the year)-but, with so much irony, ToM collapses all of this complicatedness and difference in such a way as to deny the rhetoricity, symbolicity, and empathic potentialities of numerous kinds of minds.[33]

This quote is also reminiscent of what sociologist Damian Milton has described in his paper on the double empathy problem. In this paper, he states that rather than localizing a lack of empathy in the autistic person, we need to acknowledge that people with very different experiences of the world will have difficulties in empathizing with each other. It is unfair to think that this is merely a problem of autistic people not empathizing with non-autistic people: the opposite is equally the case, perhaps even more so.[34] As ethicists, we must guard against locating deficiencies in other people too quickly, especially if they are different from us.

In this chapter, I sketched some of the explanatory models of autism and their relevance to the ethics of autism. I have described how autism has been used as an example in meta-ethics, and how specific theories have harmed autistic people. I have focused on critiques of the deficiency in Theory of Mind theory, because the theory and the critique have gained much attention during recent decades. It is possible that, in the upcoming years, the other theories will also receive critique or perhaps praise. Perhaps there is not one thing called autism, and we should not explain the origins of autism by looking at neurology but at the historical context in which it arose. The idea that autistic behaviour

---

33 Melanie Yergeau and Bryce Huebner, 'Minding Theory of Mind', *Journal of Social Philosophy*, 48:3 (2017), 273–96.

34 Damian Milton, 'On the ontological status of autism: the "double empathy problem"', *Disability & Society*, 27:6 (2012), 883–87.

should correlate with a neurological and cognitive essence that is different from typical functioning seems straightforward. However, autistic researchers themselves think more and more that there is no one definitive explanation for the differences between autistic and non-autistic functioning and that there may be 'many autisms'.[35] Perhaps some of the theories are only applicable to a subset of people diagnosed with autism. In that respect, it is helpful to look at the historical and cultural context in which autism as a concept arose. This is the topic of the next chapter, in which I discuss social-constructivist explanations of autism.

---

35   Francesca Happé, Angelica Ronald, and Robert Plomin, 'Time to give up on a single explanation for autism', *Nature Neuroscience*, 9 (2006), 1218–20.

4. Sociological and Historical Explanations of Autism

We can interpret 'understanding autism' in different ways and on different levels. In the previous chapter, I described how people have tried to explain autistic behaviour based on specific cognitive models. I explained the most prevalent of these models, and demonstrated how some philosophers have used them in particular arguments about morality. I discussed two texts that show how the explanatory model we choose also has practical and ethical consequences for how we look at responsibility. Accepting the Theory of Mind hypothesis without further reflection may lead to autistic people not being taken seriously when they speak about their own experiences. It is striking how often these theories explain the challenges that autistic people face by pointing out a deficiency in the *individual*. Just as explanations of autism that primarily point to its genetic origins, this can encourage us to consider autism first and foremost as a medical problem, to be diagnosed and solved. However, we can also explain autism differently. We can ask ourselves why autism has become so visible from the 1940s onwards, and, more specifically, during recent decades.

Cross-culturally, it seems to be the case that behaviour considered typical in children in one culture is judged elsewhere in a wholly different way. In March 2017, I attended a conference in London entitled *The Globalization of Autism*, organized by Bonnie Evans, a historian of science. There we discussed whether autism means different things in different contexts. We may wonder whether it is not colonial to use diagnostic toolkits developed in a specific cultural context to detect autism in other cultures. One researcher, Tyler Zoanni of New York University, talked about how in Uganda, the primary criterion to diagnose autism is delay or absence of speech. Other behaviours, such as not looking in adults'

  https://doi.org/10.11647/OBP.0261.04

eyes, are expected of local children and cannot be used in diagnostics. In a presentation about the history of autism in Taiwan, researcher Lai Pin Yu provided insight into the difficulties diagnosticians face when diagnosing autism in Taiwan through a Western lens. In Taiwan, speaking at a later age is not always experienced as problematic but is sometimes considered a sign that the child could be brilliant. What Western clinicians would consider an eating disorder is often not experienced as such: Taiwanese mothers have far more patience with picky eaters. What we consider a disorder that needs intervention is, therefore, dependent on time and location, as it is closely linked to what we consider to be normal behaviour.[1]

Explaining the Rise of the Phenomenon of Autism

Some have suggested explanations for the rise of diagnoses of autism that have been quickly disproven, although they had far-reaching consequences. A small study conducted by Andrew Wakefield suggested a link between autism and the vaccination for measles/ mumps/rubella (the MMR vaccine) in the 1990s. This paper, first published in *The Lancet*, was later withdrawn. Other studies debunked, once and for all, the link between autism and vaccines. Nevertheless, some people still believe that there is a causal link between the two, which resulted in an increasing number of parents choosing not to vaccinate their children. People might still believe this for many reasons. Perhaps one of them is that the first signs of autism in a young child often become apparent at approximately the same age as the vaccination is administered. The desire for a simple explanation for autism may be another reason.

Some studies have tried to demonstrate a connection between autism and particulate matter. This may lead some to conclude that the increasing number of children diagnosed is due to decreased air quality in recent decades. The assortative mating theory suggests that parents with specific joint interests, such as mathematics, science, or technology, would, by bringing together their genes, more often have children with autism.[2] Descriptions of historical figures, such as those by Uta Frith

---

1   Hyun Uk Kim, 'Autism across Cultures: Rethinking Autism', *Disability & Society*, 27:4 (2012), 535–45, https://doi.org/10.1080/09687599.2012.659463

2   Simon Baron-Cohen, 'Two New Theories of Autism: Hyper-systemising and Assortative Mating', *Archives of Disease in Childhood*, 91:1 (2006), 2–5, https://doi.org/10.1136/adc.2005.075846

in *Autism: Explaining the Enigma*, suggest that there has always been autism.[3] We are just now starting to notice it. To engage with these discussions, we must first pry some issues apart.

Firstly, there is a distinction between autism as a kind of innate personality trait and autism as a clinical diagnosis, a clinical presentation of someone who visits the (child) psychiatrist with specific challenges that need answers and solutions. We can assume that there have always been persons with certain personality traits that we would now call autistic. Still, the need to diagnose such people and give a DSM label is relatively recent. People often refer to aspects of current Western society to explain the prevalence of autism and other so-called developmental disorders such as ADHD. Social behaviour is regarded highly, and the loner with a fanatical hobby is doomed to lead a lonely life filled with misunderstanding by others. However, the fact that we live in an autismogenic society, in which an ever smaller group of smooth operators is considered normal, is in itself not a sufficient reason why the diagnosis of autism, something previously thought of as a rare paediatric disorder, has taken flight in the last decades.

Measuring Selves

In the spirit of Michel Foucault's work, the British sociologist Nikolas Rose and colleagues tried to answer a similar question in the context of psychology, neuroscience, and psychiatry in general. Rose states in his book *Inventing Our Selves: Psychology, Power and Personhood* how psychology, as a new science in the twentieth century, has invented the concept of the average individual.[4] Thus this discipline has played an essential role in engendering the terminology we use when we think about ourselves:

> For it is only at this historical moment, and in a limited and localized geographical space, that human being is understood in terms of individuals who are selves, each equipped with an inner domain, a 'psychology', which is structured by the interaction between a particular

---

3   Uta Frith, *Autism: Explaining the Enigma*, 2nd ed. (Malden, MA: Blackwell Pub, 2003).

4   Nikolas Rose, *Inventing Our Selves: Psychology, Power, and Personhood* (Cambridge: Cambridge University Press, 1998).

biographical experience and certain general laws or processes of the
human animal.[5]

Hence, according to psychology, some general rules structure how we
are selves are shaped: we can measure these processes and statistical
deviations. Because variations are now objectively measured, they
can also be named: the disorder has an objective basis, and we can
demonstrate it through measurement. The instruments of psychology
have made psychiatry into an exact science. Rose calls this 'govern[ing]
subjectivity according to norms claiming the status of science, by
professionals grounding their authority in an esoteric but objective
knowledge.'[6] Furthermore, he states that psychology becomes expertise:
'It is in this fashion that psychological ways of thinking and acting
have come to infuse the practices of other social actors such as doctors,
social workers, managers, nurses, even accountants.'[7] We can see this
mechanism also in the diagnosis of autism. Although this is a psychiatric
diagnosis, it is, in optimal circumstances, given after an extensive and
multidisciplinary investigation that includes educational scientists and
psychologists. The so-called *praecox*-feeling of the psychiatrist, a sensing
of the correct diagnosis when she first encounters her patient, is not
sufficient. The psychiatrist no longer merely relies on her expertise and
experience in attributing a diagnosis but is supported by a vast scale of
tests that substantiate the scientific validity of the diagnosis.

However, we might wonder about the relationship between what
we test (for example, autism or intelligence) and the tests themselves.
Do they test the phenomenon itself, and are they, therefore, valid?[8] Or
are we talking primarily about reliability? A measurement is reliable if,
when different people measure something, they will come to the same
conclusion. If we take the example of intelligence, we might wonder
what intelligence is: does the IQ test measure intelligence, or do we
define intelligence as the IQ test outcome? The former seems to be
problematic: IQ tests are also context-sensitive, and as there appears to

---

5   Rose, *Inventing Our Selves*, p. 23.
6   Ibid., p. 75.
7   Ibid., p. 86.
8   Denny Borsboom, Gideon J. Mellenbergh, and Jaap van Heerden, 'The
     Concept of Validity', *Psychological Review*, 111.4 (2004), 1061–71, https://doi.
     org/10.1037/0033-295X.111.4.1061

be no agreement about the ontological status of intelligence. The latter suggests that such tests are merely social constructs and conventions, without actual truth status. We could follow the same reasoning for autism. Diagnostic instruments such as ADOS-2 are based on the criteria for Autism Spectrum Disorder, as described in DSM-5.[9] Do we then test to what extent someone satisfies these criteria or to what extent someone has an underlying condition ('autism')? In later work, Nikolas Rose, together with Joelle M. Abi-Rached, has also applied these ideas to neuroscience. They argue that psychiatry has increasingly become neurology, and we think about ourselves more and more in terms of the brain. However, according to them, this does not lead to defeatist thinking about ourselves: our brain does not merely control us, but we are deemed responsible for improving ourselves, as brains, employing medical and other techniques.[10]

A Different View of Childhood

Several sociologists and philosophers of science have explored why autism appeared in the middle of the previous century. One of the first comprehensive sociological explanations of autism can be found in *Constructing Autism. Unravelling the 'Truth' and Understanding the Social* by Majia Holmer Nadesan.[11] Nadesan, a mother of a child with a diagnosis of autism, describes how autism is the result of several practices in the twentieth century. In the nineteenth century and before that, autism was unthinkable. Not only was there no such concept, but people also did not consider children as interesting enough for psychiatry or a clinic. At a particular moment, the conditions of possibility were created for autism as a phenomenon, in need of a name and a diagnosis:

> However, the question typically arising in discussions on the relationship between culture and illness (in all of its forms including mental illness)

---

9   Adam McCrimmon and Kristin Rostad, 'Test Review: Autism Diagnostic Observation Schedule, Second Edition (ADOS-2) Manual (Part II): Toddler Module', *Journal of Psychoeducational Assessment*, 32:1 (2014), 88–92, https://doi.org/10.1177/0734282913490916

10   Nikolas Rose and Joelle M. Abi-Rached, *Neuro: The New Brain Sciences and the Management of the Mind* (Princeton: Princeton University Press, 2013).

11   Majia Holmer Nadesan, *Constructing Autism: Unravelling the 'truth' and Understanding the Social* (London; New York: Routledge, 2005).

is whether the cultural component is simply built upon a foundational and determining biological component or, conversely, whether the biological component exists at all. Is culture merely the clothing within which the diseased body appears? Or, does culture-through its practices of hygiene and diet and through its medical vocabularies and institutions — produce disease in its entirety? For those versed in academic debates, one can easily recognize the eternal battle between realists in the materialist camp and nominalists in the idealist camp having their say about the nature and origins of health and disease. At issue here are the seemingly inescapable dualisms in western thought between mind and body, culture and biology.[12]

Nadesan points to an important fact here: often, a sociological or social-constructivist approach to autism is confused with a denial of the biological or phenomenological reality of autism. However, this is not what she argues (nor do I in this book). To understand a phenomenon such as autism, and to be able to reflect on it ethically and philosophically, we need to understand the different aspects of it. Nadesan investigates how autism in the first part of the twentieth century arose as a phenomenon. How is it possible that at that given moment, a pattern of behaviour did catch the attention of the medical profession? Nadesan explains this firstly by referring to the changing status of the child. Only in the nineteenth century, when child mortality was decreasing, was childhood considered to be a separate stage, qualitatively speaking, in human life. People no longer believed children should become wage-earners as soon as was practicable; rather, childhood was seen as a distinct period of one's life for which the state could set specific conditions.. In different countries, official education became compulsory. Because children were now under the scrutiny of educators, teachers, and researchers, their psyche also became an object of study. Psychoanalysis, as invented by Sigmund Freud, stressed the influence of what happens in the first years of life upon later mental development. Researchers such as Jean Piaget and later Lawrence Kohlberg dedicated their lives to studying the different phases of childhood.

Because of these developments, children became interesting for psychiatry: the clinical gaze was turned on them. Clinicians and doctors thought about normal development, and because of that, those who

---

12   Nadesan, *Constructing Autism*, pp. 21–22.

deviated from normal development stood out. In the thirties and forties, child psychiatry developed under the impulse of Leo Kanner and others, and at the same time, the diagnosis of autism was born. The concept of autism could only find acceptance from the moment that these institutions (compulsory education, child psychiatry, psychological research laying down the contours of normality) had acquired an influential role in society. Nadesan also describes how the development of computational analogies influenced the shaping of the meaning of autism. Ideas such as Theory of Mind — or the lack thereof — and the corresponding modules in our brain only work if we conceptualize our brain as a kind of central processing unit, consisting of parts that can be broken. Furthermore, although Asperger considered autism to be a personality disorder, the idea of autism as a developmental disorder has been retained. Autism is now primarily conceived as the atypical course of the biological development of a child, beginning before birth:

> The ascendancy of the cognitive paradigm thereby produced significant effects for the study of 'abnormal' child psychology. As delineated above, it led to more interest in, research about, and surveillance over very early processes of cognitive development in infants. The paradigm both telescopes for scrutiny and fragments the mind as it seeks to identify the various components of cognitive development. Accordingly, I believe it has contributed to the increased rate of diagnoses of high-functioning forms of autism including PDD, Asperger's syndrome, as well as partially explaining the increased diagnoses of ADD and ADHD (Croen et al. 2002). On the other hand, it has also destigmatized, to a certain degree, a psychological diagnosis because it replaced molar categories of normalcy and pathology with a multitude of developmental continua used to describe the acquisition of a considerable range of intellectual and social skills and abilities.[13]

The emphasis on autism being a developmental disorder also suggests that it is a medical problem. On the one hand, it is situated in the biology of individuals. On the other hand, it is responsive to interventions. In English speaking countries in particular, there is a proliferation of therapies — especially behavioural therapies — that try to bring the atypical development of the autistic child back on track.

---

13   Ibid., p. 113.

Deinstitutionalisation and Expertise

Gil Eyal and his colleagues at Columbia University in New York discuss the rise of autism diagnoses in their book *The Autism Matrix* and the article 'For a Sociology of Expertise: The Social Origins of the Autism Epidemic'.[14] They claim that this rise is due to the deinstitutionalisation of children who would previously have been considered intellectually disabled. This is partly explained by the availability of services and therapies for autism, and the fact that intellectual disability carried greater connotations of being insurmountable.[15] Eyal juxtaposes naturalistic and social-constructivist explanations. According to naturalistic explanations, there are now truly more cases of autism. Nevertheless, according to social-constructivist explanations, there are no more cases: we can explain the rise of cases by referring to the broadening of diagnostic criteria or the pressure by parents' organisations to receive a less stigmatizing diagnosis than mental retardation. Neither one of these explanations is sufficient according to Eyal, who asks: if the rise is due to a greater availability of diagnostic criteria, why were these broadened in the first place?

Eyal then turns the question around: why was autism so rare before? According to him, this is because children with an intellectual disability usually lived in institutions. There, it did not matter whether they had a diagnosis of intellectual disability or autism. At a certain point in history, parents started to take care of these children at home, and something shifted in the locus of expertise. Expertise used to be solely attributed to the child psychiatrist. Now, parents are the experts regarding their child. Eyal looks at expertise (and diagnosis) through the lens of Actor-Network Theory, as Bruno Latour and others have devised and applied it. Expertise is a network that joins professional actors, and clients and their parents together with (diagnostic) instruments and institutions. These actors work together to create and maintain a specific phenomenon: in this case, the rise of diagnoses. Parents, now they had their child at home, went looking for professionals and therapists who

---

14   Gil Eyal, 'For a Sociology of Expertise: The Social Origins of the Autism Epidemic', *American Journal of Sociology*, 118:4 (2013), 863–907, https://doi.org/10.1086/668448
15   *The Autism Matrix: The Social Origins of the Autism Epidemic*, ed. by Gil Eyal (Cambridge, UK ; Malden, MA: Polity Press, 2010).

could help them raise their child, and, while raising them, they made use of their own experiences and expertise.

For example, in *Applied Behavioural Analysis (ABA)*, a therapy based on behaviourist principles (praise and, in the earlier versions, punishment), parents were actively enrolled as therapists for their children. The therapy was so time intensive that there was no other possibility. Eyal compares this evolution with the diagnosis of childhood schizophrenia: in the sixties, this diagnosis was also on the rise. However, the prescribed treatment was a six-month stay in the hospital, together with electroshock therapy. It is understandable that this kind of therapy was not popular with parents (and probably with their children). It was also not very efficient. This may have led to the fact that ultimately the diagnosis of schizophrenia became less and less popular. Behavioural therapies developed for autism likewise have not proven their effectiveness even today, and many autistic people consider them abusive. Nevertheless, for many parents, these therapies were an acceptable and understandable way to help their children, and they at least seemed practical.

Moreover, parents felt that they did not just impose the treatment on their children. They worked together with the child to improve the challenges that the family were experiencing. This might explain why parents more readily accept autism as a diagnosis. Furthermore, Eyal mentions the rise of self-advocacy: the stories of autistic adults who can talk knowledgeably about their own functioning, such as Temple Grandin. Because these adults became known to the general public, people could see autism as a different way of being, with which it is possible to live a fulfilling life. Eyal suggests that such examples of self-reliant adults have contributed to the fact that parents chose autism above so-called mental retardation as a diagnosis.

Shifting Autism

Maija Nadesan and Gil Eyal have tried to explain the birth and the expansion of autism as a diagnostic category. On the one hand, a different view of childhood was dawning. On the other hand, relations between parents and professionals were changing. However, we can ask ourselves whether, throughout the history of the concept of autism, we are talking about the same phenomenon. Berend Verhoeff, a Dutch psychiatrist and philosopher, investigates this question in several publications.[16] In 'Autism in Flux: a History of the Concept from Leo Kanner to DSM-5',[17] he describes that the concept of autism as something that has expanded throughout history, but that fundamentally can be brought back to autism as described by Kanner and Asperger, is not correct. The idea of autism as a continuous phenomenon results from a rewriting of history by autism professionals. In research as well as in diagnostic practice, Verhoeff states, we often assume that autism is a natural essence that we can discover: the more biomedical research we do, the closer we will come to the truth of autism. He ascribes the idea of a discoverable essence of autism to the fact that autism professionals always interpret the history of autism in the light of that one essence.

Verhoeff suggests, however, that the diagnosis has not expanded, but that we are now talking about a different phenomenon from the one in Kanner's time. Kanner talks about extreme autistic aloneness. This may not be the same as experiencing challenges in social functioning or communication. In the first twenty years after Kanner's first paper about autism, his definition persisted: autistic children were aloof, extremely alone and insistent on sameness. However, later on, under the influence of developments in cognitive sciences and the idea that language is a code, autism came to be considered more and more as a communication problem. Autistic people had difficulties understanding the symbolism of language. Under Lorna Wing's influence in the eighties, issues with social interaction came to the foreground again. However, these issues were not the same as Kanner's autistic aloneness but referred to challenges in understanding the unwritten laws of social interaction. According to Verhoeff, these are two different things. It is probable, Verhoeff states, that we cannot talk about autism as a condition about which we gradually learn more, but about a shift in what we mean by

---

16 Berend Verhoeff, 'The autism puzzle: challenging a mechanistic model on conceptual and historical grounds,' *Philos Ethics Humanit Med*, 8:17 (2013), https://doi.org/10.1186/1747-5341-8-17; Berend Verhoeff, 'Fundamental Challenges for Autism Research: The Science-Practice Gap, Demarcating Autism and the Unsuccessful Search for the Neurobiological Basis of Autism', *Medicine, Health Care, and Philosophy*, 18:3 (2015), 443–47, https://doi.org/10.1007/s11019-015-9636-7

17 Berend Verhoeff, 'Autism in Flux: A History of the Concept from Leo Kanner to DSM-5', *History of Psychiatry*, 24:4 (2013), 442–58, https://doi.org/10.1177/0957154X13500584

autism. The children that Kanner described may have had a different disorder from those who receive this diagnosis today.

Abandoning the Label

How should we respond to the idea that autism as a phenomenon is dependent on time and place, and that it may not refer to a single biological essence that we can discover if we look hard enough? Autism researcher Lynn Waterhouse suggests that we should stop using 'autism' as a concept in research: autism is a description of two symptoms that happen to occur together, but that do not correspond to an underlying biological cause that we can research. Research that tries to find the neurological, genetic or cognitive explanation is hence doomed to fail.[18] Does this mean that it does not make sense anymore to use autism as a diagnostic label? Maybe we have to look for something that approaches the underlying biological truth more closely, and start using that in the clinic. Alternatively, perhaps we should stop labelling children with disorders such as autism. The British psychiatrist Sami Timimi thinks so. Together with Neil Gardner and Brian McCabe, two adults who rejected their autism or Asperger syndrome diagnoses, he wrote *The Myth of Autism: Medicalising Men's and Boys' Social and Emotional Competence.*[19] In this book, the authors argue that we should abandon the concept of autism, as it is not based on scientific fact. In the paper 'Children's Mental Health: Time to Stop Using Psychiatric Diagnoses,'[20] he follows the same line. There is no proof of a biological cause of autism, and the effectiveness of existing therapies is not proven either. On the contrary, labelling leads to stigmatisation and medicalisation. We should no longer try to diagnose children with labels that are not supported by scientific proof. We have to engage in a different form of clinical practice,

---

18 Lynn Waterhouse, Lynn Eric London, and Christopher Gillberg, 'ASD Validity', *Review Journal of Autism and Developmental Disorders* (2016), 1–28; Lynn Waterhouse, *Rethinking Autism: Variation and Complexity* (Cambridge: Academic Press, 2013).

19 Sami Timimi, Neil Gardner, and Brian McCabe, *The Myth of Autism: Medicalising Men's and Boys' Social and Emotional Competence* (London: Macmillan Education UK, 2010).

20 Sami Timimi, 'Children's Mental Health: Time to Stop Using Psychiatric Diagnosis', *European Journal of Psychotherapy & Counselling*, 17:4 (2015), 342–58, https://doi.org /10.1080/13642537.2015.1094500

one that puts the experiences and feedback of clients at the centre and looks at them in their specific contexts.

This chapter has explored how autism as a phenomenon in the clinic arose over the last century. Although the kinds of people we now call autistic may always have existed, they have been given this specific diagnosis only recently. Moreover, autism is a biologically heterogeneous condition. It may be impossible to find one specific biological cause. This has led scholars such as Sami Timimi to reject DSM diagnoses such as autism in the clinic. They argue that there is no reason to keep diagnoses that can lead to stigma and have no underlying biological essence.

Nevertheless, many adults with a recent diagnosis of autism claim that this diagnosis helps them, gives them insight into their everyday functioning and allows them finally to understand themselves. Autism is real as a shared experience for autistic adults and for parents and psychiatrists. We can concede that the phenotype of autism is heterogeneous, perhaps even on a biological level, but that it is at the same time recognizable. Moreover, the concept of autism creates a common language that is understandable and recognizable for those diagnosed and for those in their environment. We could also consider autism as a disability, one that is not straightforwardly associated with lesser wellbeing but that is an integral part of one's identity. In the next chapter, we will explore concepts of disability and suggest how these can accommodate diverse experiences.

PART II: EXPERIENCES OF AUTISM

Life is Experience – George Canguilhem

5. Difference and Disability

In the previous chapters, we have described autism as a phenomenon for which different neurocognitive explanations may be applicable. We have also seen how autism may have had different meanings throughout history and in different cultures. For example, in the second half of the previous century, it became more widespread and associated with a cognitive disability. Today, some people still make the distinction between those autistics with a cognitive disability, who have challenges functioning autonomously (sometimes called 'low-functioning' or even 'severe autism'), and those without a cognitive disability (sometimes called 'high-functioning'). Indeed, one of the more challenging aspects of studying the ethics of autism is being confronted with fierce discussions online between some parents of autistic children and some autistic adults. Parents of autistic children sometimes reproach autistic adults, many of them neurodiversity advocates, that they cannot speak for their child: their child, so it goes, has severe challenges, needs medical help, and according to some, even a cure. Neurodiversity proponents object that their experiences can be informative and can help understand children who are perhaps intellectually disabled and do not speak. They say that even in the case of children whom people might think of as 'severely autistic', autism is not something to be cured, and we should not subject children to behavioural therapies such as Applied Behavioural Analysis (ABA). Some people, however, suggest that neurodiversity is all well and good for autistic people who can speak and reason. However, children unable to speak and with learning difficulties are considered much worse off and in need of therapy and treatment.

These debates are philosophically challenging. We might ask ourselves on what basis we can say that a specific type of person is better off than others. It may be the case that verbal autistics with an average or above-average intelligence appear more 'typical' and better

    https://doi.org/10.11647/OBP.0261.05

functioning than children with a much lower score on an IQ test. For example, in mainstream bioethics, scholars have often assumed that IQ and wellbeing or even happiness are intrinsically linked. However, as I shall point out, this association is not without its flaws. Also problematic is the assumption that those autistics with an average or above-average intelligence are automatically better off in terms of wellbeing and therefore should only marginally contribute to the debate about autism. The testimony from of this group of people sometimes expresses great suffering. In this chapter, I will resist the temptation to associate a good life with higher intelligence or with being able to function autonomously. This is equally so for non-verbal autistic people as for so-called 'high-functioning' autistics who speak for themselves: I think we cannot take it at face value that the former are more in need of 'therapy or treatment' than the latter. Instead, we should learn from disability studies that we must take first-person perspectives seriously and shy away from easy assumptions about wellbeing and happiness based on broad categories such as intelligence. In general, we can challenge the association between being more 'typical' or 'normal' and wellbeing, and acknowledge that advocating for and establishing a culture that accepts atypicality may bring us a long way.

Up till now, I have discussed autism in different ways. I have described it as a diagnosis on the rise, a psychiatric disorder, and a neurological reality. At the same time, autism is often called a disability. I have put aside the fact that this is not the case in all countries. In states with a robust psychoanalytic tradition, such as France and Brazil, it is often not customary to diagnose children first and then treat them: clinicians usually deem a diagnosis unnecessary to provide therapy.[1] Moreover, we can distinguish between mental illness and a disability (cognitive or not): how a particular condition is perceived can have far-reaching consequences for treatment. Furthermore, because in these countries autism is often considered to be a mental illness, it is treated with psychoanalytic therapies. In places that approach it as a disability, the treatment is given with this in mind. Autistic children

---

1   Francisco Ortega, Rafaela Zorzanelli, and Clarice Rios, 'The Biopolitics of Autism in Brazil', in *Re-Thinking Autism. Diagnosis, Identity and Equality*, ed. by Katherine Runswick-Cole, Rebecca Mallett, and Sami Timimi (London and Philadelphia: Jessica Kingsley Publishers, 2016), pp. 19–19.

receive behavioural therapy, or they are offered psycho-education. Many parents, therefore, oppose psychoanalytic therapy in these countries and strive to have autism labelled as a disability. The treatment of autism in the psychoanalytic tradition is beyond the scope of this book. In Belgium, policymakers consider autism a disability, and services and autism support are dealt with in the same way as services and support for other disabilities.

Disability and Bioethics

Before we return to the question of autism, it is useful to reflect on disabilities and the status that disability has in our ethical considerations. Bioethicists investigate cases related to prenatal screening, and editing and selecting in-vitro embryos. Unavoidably the question about the wellbeing of people with a disability arises here. Utilitarian thinkers such as Julian Savulescu argue that it is better to be born without a disability than with one.[2] Prospective parents therefore have reason, should they have the choice, to choose an embryo without a disability. Along the same lines, one could argue that pregnant mothers, if confronted with the fact that their foetus has a chromosomal, genetic, or other abnormality that could lead to a disability such as Down syndrome, might be best advised to choose prenatal screening and termination of the pregnancy.

As a postdoctoral researcher, I spent some time reflecting on whether we ought to know the complete genome of in-vitro embryos, and, based on that, select the 'best' embryo. The existing bioethics literature extensively dealt with Savulescu's principle of procreative beneficence. After all, who can deny that if you know that one embryo has a disability and the other one has not, it is not better to choose the latter? According to some philosophers, such as John Harris, it is even better not to let embryos with a disability be born, even if there is no embryo without a disability available.[3] In these discussions, having a disability is always automatically linked with lesser wellbeing. Often this is done

---

2   Julian Savulescu, 'Procreative Beneficence: Why We Should Select the Best Children', *Bioethics*, 15:5–6 (2001), 413–26; Julian Savulescu and Guy Kahane, 'The Moral Obligation to Create Children with the Best Chance of the Best Life', *Bioethics*, 23 (2009), 274–90, https://doi.org/10.1111/j.1467-8519.2008.00687.x

3   John Harris, 'One Principle and Three Fallacies of Disability Studies', *Journal of Medical Ethics*, 27:6 (2001), 383–87, https://doi.org/10.1136/jme.27.6.383

with reference to common sense. It seems self-evident that it is better to be born without physical or cognitive disabilities and that having such disabilities reduces the wellbeing of those involved. However, these intuitions may be misguided. Such assumptions can be tested with empirical studies. And indeed, empirical studies into people's wellbeing in general, and more specifically, people with a disability, have been extensively conducted. Down syndrome is a standard case. Many pregnancy terminations undertaken for medical reasons happen because the foetus has trisomy-21, the extra chromosome 21 that causes Down syndrome. Concerns about the wellbeing of the child could play a role here. Nevertheless, the empirical research of Brian Skotko and others has demonstrated that people with Down syndrome do not, by definition, have lower wellbeing. Their parents or brothers and sisters are often not unhappier than the parents and siblings of children without Down syndrome.[4]

Even more striking are the results of a study into the wellbeing of boys with Duchenne Muscular Dystrophy. Although it is clear that these boys suffer from a devastating disease, that they often become unable to walk at a young age and will die young, they report that they have a relatively high quality of life.[5] I give these examples not as a plea against pregnancy termination but as an illustration that it is common to give a simplistic view in present-day bioethical discussions about what it means to have a disability. In her book, *Disability Bioethics*, Jackie Leach Scully has already pointed this out.[6] She provides us with an explanation that bioethicists are asked to evaluate new medical technologies ethically. Hence, they have a symbiotic relationship with

---

4   Brian G. Skotko, and Susan P. Levine, 'What the Other Children Are Thinking: Brothers and Sisters of Persons with Down Syndrome', *American Journal of Medical Genetics. Part C, Seminars in Medical Genetics*, 142C (2006), 180–86; Brian G. Skotko, Susan P. Levine, and Richard Goldstein, 'Having a Son or Daughter with Down Syndrome: Perspectives from Mothers and Fathers', *American Journal of Medical Genetics. Part A*, 155A (2011), 2335–47; Brian G. Skotko, Susan P. Levine, and Richard Goldstein, 'Self-Perceptions from People with Down Syndrome', *American Journal of Medical Genetics. Part A*, 155A (2011), 2360–69.

5   Saskia L. S. Houwen-van Opstal, Merel Jansen, Nens Van Alfen, Imelda de Groot, 'Health-Related Quality of Life and Its Relation to Disease Severity in Boys with Duchenne Muscular Dystrophy: Satisfied Boys, Worrying Parents — a Case-Control Study', *Journal of Child Neurology*, 29:11 (2014), 1486–95, https://doi.org/10.1177/0883073813506490

6   Jackie Leach Scully, *Disability Bioethics: Moral Bodies, Moral Difference* (Plymouth: Rowman & Littlefield, 2008).

the biomedical world. Therefore, she states that many bioethicists use the conceptual framework of medicine to think about disabilities: they see disabilities as impairments in individuals that need fixing. Bioethicists would be best also to use insights from disability studies in their considerations.[7] On the question of termination of pregnancy, this does not mean that we need to replace one straightforward answer (best to terminate) with another one. Prospective parents may have many different reasons to terminate a pregnancy of a disabled foetus. For example, in the case of Duchenne Muscular Dystrophy, they may find the idea of losing a son at a young age unbearable. What we should challenge, however, is the automatic association between disability and a lower quality of life.

Models of Disability

When we talk about disability, often a distinction is made between the medical and the social model of disability. According to the medical model of disability, it is assumed that disability exists within the individual and that we have to try to eliminate it with medical treatments. According to the social model of disability, physical or cognitive impairments are neutral: they become a disability because of society's lack of support. In an ideal world, impairments do not become disabilities. The Convention on the Rights of Persons with Disabilities assumes the social model and lays down the rights of people with a disability.[8] They have a right to integrate into society fully and to have equal opportunity in education and labour. Still, some have criticized specific interpretations of the social model of disability. This model sometimes ignores the experience of the person with a particular impairment. The emphasis is on external social powers that render

---

7   I would like to add that some doctors have pointed out to me several times that they believe that this interpretation of medicine and medical is too one-sided. They do not only see themselves as professionals who localize illnesses or disabilities in individuals, and that pathologise individuals. Considering individuals in their broader context is also an integral part of the medical profession.

8   Jackie Leach Scully, 'The Convention on the Rights of Persons with Disabilities and Cultural Understandings of Disability', in *Disability and Universal Human Rights: Legal, Ethical and Conceptual Implications of the Convention on the Rights of Persons with Disabilities*, ed. by Joel Anderson and Jos Philips (Utrecht: Netherlands Institute of Human Rights (SIM), 2012), pp. 71–83.

someone *disabled*, and there is not much attention paid to what it means to live in a specific body or with a particular mind. The term disability is also interpreted negatively: it is the negative result of the social context not being adapted to a specific person's impairments. In her book *The Minority Body*, Elizabeth Barnes argues for a different view: disability is not good or bad, but value-neutral.[9] You cannot say that someone, because they have a disability, is, by definition, worse off than someone else. It is, of course, possible that for some people with a disability, this disability has an impact on his or her wellbeing. However, having a disability is neutral concerning wellbeing, and having a disability can have good and bad associations. Barnes defines disability as having a minority body, a body that is different from the general norm. 'Disability' as a category of diverse phenomena is socially constructed; the specific disabilities are not. It is, of course, possible that you have a body that is in the minority and that this in itself can lead to oppression, stigma and lower wellbeing. Nevertheless, in the end, particular disabilities do not tell you much about the wellbeing of a person with the disability.

Maybe it is ultimately impossible to find the one right way to look at a disability. Disability scholar Leni Van Goidsenhoven argues that it is better to bring together different aspects of disability; disability is something physical or cognitive, but at the same time cultural. People with a disability form a minority and are oppressed by existing structures. Nevertheless, besides that, they are also individuals with a specific body, with strengths and challenges. That is precisely the reason why we should engage with both positive and negative experiences of people with a disability. Van Goidsenhoven refers to Alison Kafer's book *Feminist, Crip, Queer*,[10] and the concept of Crip Theory: an activist and at the same time theoretical view on disability. The hard word 'crip' is used deliberately.[11] Instead of trying to situate disability in the social or the medical realm, it becomes, according to Kafer, 'a set of practices and associations that can be critiqued, contested and transformed.' Because we do not take for granted a fixed model to look at disabilities, disabilities

---

9   Elizabeth Barnes, *The Minority Body: A Theory of Disability* (Oxford: Oxford University Press, 2016).

10   Alison Kafer, *Feminist, Queer, Crip* (Bloomington: Indiana University Press, 2013), p. 9.

11   Leni Van Goidsenhoven, *Autisme in veelvoud: het potentieel van life writing voor alternatieve vormen van subjectiviteit* (Antwerp: Maklu, 2020).

and persons with disabilities can, according to Van Goidsenhoven, not be caught by fixed, unmovable, and straightforward definitions, but are open, transformable, and debatable, making room for 'polysemous reading' and 'productive uncertainty'. [12]

The text *Reading Rosie* by Dan Goodley and Katherine Runswick-Cole illustrates how different ways of looking at disability are possible and how these different discourses exist next to each other. [13] The text describes, from a poststructuralist view, an eleven-year-old girl with a disability. She is 'being read' by way of four different discourses of disability that are juxtaposed. These discourses are the autism canon, the traditional social model of disability, the Scandinavian relational model of disability, and one filtered by the socio-cultural lens of the present-day child in the digital age. The authors wonder what these different discourses convey about Rosie. They state that it is not their aim to come to a more profound truth about Rosie. Instead, they want to make explicit how different stories about one child are possible, a child who is perhaps all too often reduced to her diagnosis and challenges.

Since she was three, Rosie has had an autism diagnosis as well as learning difficulties. The first reading of Rosie is based on the medical model of autism, which the authors call the autism canon. In this reading, Rosie is someone with a 'devastating disorder', a 'neurological disorder'. In this reading, children such as Rosie have deficient social skills, and they are defined by problems with their language and repetitive behaviour. According to this model, we can explain Rosie's interest in photography by her autism, through which she is more interested in technical objects than in other people. Indeed, so-called restricted interests are part of the diagnostic criteria for autism. I remember taking an online course in autism diagnosis geared at psychologists and clinical professionals. At a certain point, the instructor gave the following example: 'if a five-year-old boy knows a few names of dinosaurs, this is normal. If a five-year-old boy knows all the dinosaurs' names, an alarm should go off. Even more so if he is not interested in dinosaurs, but say drainpipes, and knows everything about them.' I thought this was a somewhat restricted view of what should be considered typical interests in children. Maybe

---

12 Van Goidsenhoven, *Autisme in veelvoud.*
13 Dan Goodley and Katherine Runswick-Cole, 'Reading Rosie: The Postmodern Dis/Abled Child,' *Educational and Child Psychology*, 29:2 (2012), 53–66.

we could see the particular interest of the drainpipe-loving boy as refreshing and original. Who knows how exciting drainpipes can be! In a 2005 paper, Dinah Murray, Wenn Lawson, and Mike Lesser have called this the monotropic mind: a focus on a small number of interests at any time, therefore sometimes missing things outside of the attention tunnel.[14] However, it is hard to see how having a few restricted interests is more pathological than a mind that wanders.

The second reading in *Reading Rosie* is that of the social model of disability. Disability in this reading is not an individual medical disorder but the result of a disabling society that does not consider the needs of people with specific impairments. Disability is social oppression. In this reading, children with a particular disability, such as Rosie, are more often the victim of social oppression: she is being stared at when she exhibits behaviour that does not fit expectations and follows leisurely activities in a specialized centre. The third reading is that of the Scandinavian relational model of disability. This model defines disability as a mismatch between a person's capabilities and the functional demands of the context. Disability exists in relation to the environment. A blind person is not disabled when she has to make a telephone call, and not at all in a dark environment. By looking at disability relationally, the conditions of possibility are created for empowerment: adjustments to the living environment make it possible for a disabled person to flourish. In this reading, Rosie is a happy and playful child when she is at home. If people she does not know visit, she finds that problematic: she prefers to be in a quiet and predictable environment. Her disability thus only becomes apparent when there is a mismatch between Rosie and her surroundings.

In the last reading, the authors describe Rosie as a 'typical child of the digital age': at one point, one of the researchers brought a camera, and Rosie used this immediately and with much gusto. She took pictures of favourite objects and in this way she showed her interests and the things she loves. All these readings show us different aspects of what disability, in this case, autism, can mean: a lens through which your interests are interpreted, a form of social oppression, but also — in the last example — as a child with her own interests and a life-world

---

14 Dinah Murray, Mile Lesser, Wendy Lawson, 'Attention, monotropism and the diagnostic criteria for autism', *Autism* 9:2 (May 2005), 139–56.

apart from the label, with a rich family life in which she flourishes. By looking at Rosie through these different narratives, we gain a broader view of what disability can mean and how a simple view on disability, using one model only, can reduce a person to a medical disorder or the product of social oppression. If we want to understand what disability is, we should not limit ourselves to one model. Instead, we should think of these models together to grasp the complexity and polysemy of the phenomenon. In the case of *Reading Rosie,* it may have been good to add a further reading: the story that Rosie would tell herself about her interests and experiences. Rosie is, in the first place, an individual with her own identity and her own experiences.

Neurodiversity and Disability

Most scholars of disability studies have investigated physical disabilities, as in the book mentioned earlier by Elizabeth Barnes. The idea of a neutral deviation from the typical is also apparent in the neurodiversity movement. For a good overview and contemporary interpretation of neurodiversity, I recommend philosopher Robert Chapman's work.[15] Although the neurodiversity movement is itself diverse, and one description cannot cover all of its manifestations, neurodiversity advocates reject the idea of autism as an illness or disorder. They would probably appreciate the value-free concept of disability that Barnes proposes. Indeed, they often vehemently oppose the frequent biomedical assumption that autism is a disorder that needs to be solved, treated or cured. Still, if a person ignorant about current discussions about neurodiversity and disability visited a large conference for autism researchers such as INFAR, it would be hard to shake the impression that autism must be a disease. Researchers refer to their autistic participants with the term 'patients', genetic causes are actively sought

---

15   See: Robert Chapman, 'Neurodiversity, Disability, Wellbeing', in *Neurodiversity Studies: A New Critical Paradigm*, ed. by Nick Chown, Anna Stenning, Hanna Rosquvist (London: Routledge, 2020), pp. 57–72; Robert Chapman, 'The Reality of Autism: on the metaphysics of disorder and diversity', *Philosophical Psychology* (2019), 799–819; Robert Chapman, 'Neurodiversity Theory and its Discontents: Autism, Schizophrenia, and the Social Model', in *The Bloomsbury Companion to the Philosophy of Psychiatry*, ed. by Serife Tekin, Robyn Bluhm (London: Bloomsbury, 2019), pp. 371–90.

after, and mouse models are created to track these causes and develop pharmacogenetic treatments. However, is 'illness' the proper term to use when we talk about autism?

Philosopher Christopher Mole has argued that whether autism is a disease is an ill-posed question. We should not try to answer it with a yes or a no; we should not ask the question. He admits that classifying autism as a disease has certain advantages. Such classification can contribute to the fact that the everyday challenges that autistic people encounter are taken seriously. It can also mean that we absolve people with a diagnosis of autism for behaviour that might be socially awkward. Autism then functions as a mitigating circumstance. Nevertheless, if we use the term 'illness' when talking about autism, we bundle together the mitigating circumstances and the search for a cure semantically. Such a move might be the right thing to do for somatic, non-psychiatric conditions, Mole argues, but not for psychiatric conditions. Therefore, he concludes, the question of whether autism is an illness should not be posed at all because, if you do it, you combine a set of norms that cannot properly be connected.[16]

In their article 'Autism, Neurodiversity and Equality Beyond the Normal,' Andrew Fenton and Tim Krahn investigate the concept of neurodiversity.[17] They point out that in general, and also in nature, neurological variation is far more common than is generally assumed, and this does not always lead to specific challenges.[18] On the contrary, such challenges are caused mainly by external factors. Hence we should, according to the authors, reconceptualise high-functioning autism as a normal variation. They therefore, conclude the following:

> From these observations we can conclude that, unless the relevant deficits qualify as dysfunctions (i.e., are maladaptive), the given cognitive and accompanying neurological differences—even when these are associated

---

16 Christopher Mole, 'Autism and "Disease": The Semantics of an Ill-Posed Question', *Philosophical Psychology*, 30:8 (2017), 1126–40, https://doi.org/10.1080/09515089.201 7.1338341

17 Andrew Fenton and Tim Krahn, 'Autism, Neurodiversity, and Equality beyond the "Normal"', *Journal of Ethics in Mental Health*, 2:2 (2007), 1–6.

18 We can even state, as a neurologist once said to me when he heard me use the words neurotypical and neurodiverse, that all people are neurologically different from each other. By using these terms we introduce a difference that can no longer be proven purely based on brains. It is the users of these terms, not the brains themselves, that define what can be called diverse and what typical.

with deficits in skilled behaviour—are not ordinarily grounds for pathologizing a certain way of engaging with the world.

Fenton and Krahn suggest that this may be difficult for other types of autism (so-called 'low-functioning autism'). Still, they indicate that in these cases too, it is perhaps possible to view differences as neutral. Reconceptualising autism as a neutral difference has a number of consequences: autistic people do not, by definition, need to be 'cured', and autism is not necessarily synonymous with suffering. We should look beyond our understanding of what it means to lead a good life and not only use the 'neurotypical'[19] standard. Furthermore, the authors conclude that persons diagnosed with autism should decide what they will accept as therapy and whether they need treatment.

Piers Jaarsma and Stellan Welin have elaborated on the concept of autism as a neutral difference in several papers.[20] For them, autism, and then mainly in the form of Asperger syndrome, is a neutral genetic difference involving average or high intelligence. Just like homosexuality, Asperger syndrome is not an illness or a medical problem that has to be cured, but a form of diversity and a part of someone's identity that we have to accept. Although this is a positive and emancipatory approach, there are some difficulties with it. Just as with a purely medical approach to autism, this approach stresses biological difference: autism as a different brain and different genes. It is a difference in the individual, not a mismatch between the individual or a disorder at a specific moment in the individual's development. Moreover, they also distinguish between 'high-functioning' and 'low-functioning' autism when discussing how we appreciate autism as a neutral identity. As I will discuss later on, this distinction may not hold.

---

19 'Neurotypical' in the context of autism and other phenomena, is an adjective used to refer to a person with an average neurological or psychological development, without a diagnosis of autism, ADHD, Tourette or a learning disability.

20 Pier Jaarsma and Stellan Welin, 'Autism as a Natural Human Variation: Reflections on the Claims of the Neurodiversity Movement', *Health Care Analysis*, 20:1 (2012), 20–30; Pier Jaarsma and Stellan Welin, 'Human Capabilities, Mild Autism, Deafness and the Morality of Embryo Selection', *Medicine, Health Care and Philosophy: A European Journal*, 16:4 (2013), 817–24.

Autism and Identity

Perhaps merely pointing at intrinsic and natural causes of difference, be that difference neutral or not, does not adequately reflect how complex autism is, nor the fact that it is also an identity that we can accept or reject. Moreover, such a purely individual-biological approach always carries the risk that people will see autism as a medical problem to be cured. Biology in itself is not proof that something is either a neutral or a pathological variant. The comparison with homosexuality, as suggested by Jaarsma and Welin, is promising, however. Homosexuality has been viewed for an extended period in western culture as a moral problem. Some people who tend to fall in love with people of the same gender welcomed the mention of homosexuality in the diagnostic handbook. If it is an innate condition, people cannot blame you for being gay. This is reminiscent of how an autism diagnosis sometimes functions. If you receive a diagnosis, you no longer have to comply with unattainable normality standards. The diagnosis objectively determines that the person diagnosed is different from other people and that they cannot transcend this difference through effort.

Fortunately, homosexuality has been removed from the DSM for quite some time. It is now something with which one identifies, a part of one's own identity, not something a psychiatrist detects or diagnoses. However, with Michel Foucault, we can acknowledge that it is precisely the idea of belonging to a minority that makes homosexuality function as an identity. We could imagine a world where sexual preference does not even need a name because it is considered unimportant and indeed not of moral relevance. Perhaps we can also imagine a world where specific cognitive differences do not need a name because people do not consider them relevant or they are not associated with challenges. Still, this is not what many neurodiversity activists would argue for. Most of them do not often propose that autism, as a term, should eventually disappear when society has changed to accommodate their needs better. Perhaps this is because they consider autism to be an integral part of their own identity. Nevertheless, it is precisely the idea of identity that risks being buried by an approach that puts too much stress on the biological aspects.

Suppose autism is a neutral neurological and genetic difference. In that case, there is no reason why we should not determine this as early as possible and communicate this to the child and her parents. This is indeed the direction many autism professionals would want to take. They often assume that early detection of autism is best practice, not (only) because this means it is possible to intervene early, but also because the child can be understood and supported as early as possible. However, if we introduce the comparison with homosexuality, it is not often suggested that we should detect this as early as possible. Although it is generally assumed that homosexuality is something with which you are born, and it is for the most part 'in your genes', not many people suggest that we should screen children as early as possible, should this be possible. Such an approach could, just as is argued in the context of autism, have some advantages. Early on, children would not have to be confused about their own sexual identity during adolescence because it would have already been objectively established when they were small. Still, this approach is not without problems.

On the one hand, this has to do with the fact that sexual orientation may not play a significant role in young children's lives. On the other hand, it also may have to do with the fact that we probably believe that sexual orientation is something that we should detect about ourselves and that we should assimilate into our thinking about ourselves, even though it is, of course, biologically based. Perhaps the same is true for autism. Many children are diagnosed at a young age, which can help the parents and the children themselves. But suppose autism is also an identity, besides a biological reality. In that case, this may also mean that forming, accepting, and assimilating this identity is something that the autistic person should do herself. It is not merely knowledge about one's biology. This, at least, suggests that adolescents or adults who were diagnosed as young children could redefine what autism means to them. Simply because a specific characteristic or behaviour is also in your biology, does not mean that it cannot simultaneously be an identity. Perhaps we can consider biology and identity together, without reducing one to another.

Of course, we can also ask ourselves whether we can, in all cases, think of autism as a neutral difference. It may be helpful, using the analogy with homosexuality, to imagine a society where autistic people are not considered to be different and do not need a label or diagnosis. The question remains whether this is possible for all autistic people. Some autistic people themselves state that their way of being is the cause of suffering. This suffering may even be intrinsic to their functioning regardless of the support they receive. For example, some autistic people have testified how sensory overload or sleeping problems impact their wellbeing and how they believe this is something that any support cannot help. Although most autistic people reject a cure for autism, as it is tightly linked to their identity, some would welcome a medical solution for some of its symptoms. If we only give voice to autistic people who do not experience this, that could also be considered a case of epistemic injustice, a concept that I shall describe further in the next chapter.

The discussion around self-diagnosis is also interesting. Can people diagnose themselves as autistic, just as we do not need a doctor to identify as queer? This question has led to much controversy in the autistic community. Some argue that autism has to be determined by medical professionals because only they have the relevant scientific knowledge. Those who advocate for self-diagnosis do so for several reasons. Firstly, in many parts of the world, an official diagnosis remains unattainable, and many people do not have the resources to pay for such diagnoses. Secondly, they wish to counter the medical view of autism, and stress the expertise of those living with the condition. Accordingly, they consider autism more of a neurological identity than a medical diagnosis, an identity that you can discover and define for yourself without needing a doctor's help.[21]

Still, if we talk about autism as a specific identity, one that perhaps entails particular challenges in a society that is not always accepting, how does this relate to people who experience severe challenges because of their autism, or to parents of children with severe behavioural problems? Jaarsma and Welin explicitly describe the situation of people with so-called 'high-functioning autism' and Asperger syndrome and state that those autistic people who do not belong in these categories may have a disability that cannot be thought of as a neutral variant. They, therefore, oppose the fact that in DSM-5, Asperger syndrome is no longer a separate diagnosis and falls under the umbrella of Autism

---

21   Jennifer C. Sarrett, 'Biocertification and Neurodiversity: The Role and Implications of Self-Diagnosis in Autistic Communities', *Neuroethics*, 9:1 (2016), 23–36, https://doi.org/10.1007/s12152-016-9247-x

Spectrum Disorder. However, narrowly defining autism as a 'different but neutral identity' only for well-spoken people with a high IQ test score may be a bit short-sighted. In the paper 'Advocacy, Autism and Autonomy', David DeVidi questions the distinction between 'high-functioning' and 'low-functioning' autistics. He thinks it is wrong that if people talk about the autonomy of autistic persons, they mostly only deal with the former. Many autistic persons do not use oral language, and we often overlook their point of view. Perhaps we assume too quickly that those who do not speak, or who exhibit behaviour that is not what we are accustomed to are not autonomous at all. [22]

Raffaele Rodogno, Katrin Krause-Jensen and Richard Ashcroft have discussed in their paper 'Autism and the Good Life' that it may very well be the case that some autistic people do not conceive of wellbeing in the same way non-autistic people do. Therefore, they advocate an autism-sensitive or neurodiverse-sensitive epistemology of wellbeing.[23] Ingrid Robeyns has argued in her paper 'Conceptualizing wellbeing for autistic persons' that a capabilities approach to autism, which looks at the real opportunities that society should offer autistic people, is promising, provided that the lived experiences of autistic people are taken into account, and that conflicts between the capabilities of autistics and those of their carers are avoided.[24] We may indeed not have enough knowledge about what it means to have an intellectual disability or be less autonomous. Many of the conclusions we draw are based on our own experiences. We do not have sufficient data from autistic people who cannot use oral language to talk about their own experiences and what they value in life. Does this automatically mean that autism is not an identity for them but an illness? Or even an ill identity? One of the significant challenges of the ethics of autism is that it will have to incorporate the experiences and wishes of those who do not readily talk about these things. Empirical studies with non-verbal autistic

---

22 David DeVidi, 'Advocacy, Autism and Autonomy', in *The Philosophy of Autism*, ed. by Jami L. Anderson and Simon Cushing (Lanham: Rowman & Littlefield, 2013), pp. 187–200.

23 Raffaele Rodogno, Katrin Krause-Jensen, & Richard Ashcroft, '"Autism and the good life": A new approach to the study of well-being', *Journal of Medical Ethics*, 42:6 (2016), 401–08.

24 Ingrid Robeyns, 'Conceptualising Well-Being for Autistic Persons', *Journal of Medical Ethics* 42:6, (2016), 383–90.

participants into what it means to be autonomous and its relationship to wellbeing are long overdue.

In this chapter, I have described different meanings of disability and introduced the neurodiversity approach. I have argued that we cannot subdivide autistic people based on criteria of functioning alone to draw ethical conclusions. Indeed, philosophers and ethicists need to look very carefully at their intuitions regarding concepts of autonomy and what it means to lead a good life. We must think beyond our own experiences as trained intellectuals. We may define autism, in all its forms, perhaps using an analogy with Elizabeth Barnes' minority body, as a minority brain. In this way, we do not have to deny that some autistic people suffer from some aspects related to autism. Nevertheless, we also acknowledge that this does not necessarily have to be so. Simultaneously, a poststructuralist approach such as *Reading Rosie* demonstrates that people with specific disabilities can always 'be read' in different ways, using various stories that can be juxtaposed but do not have to annihilate one another. The different meanings and dimensions of the concept of autism can then appear as in a kaleidoscope: each time we look, it is different but equally valid. Part of this endeavour is taking the experiences of autistic people seriously. In the next chapter, I shall describe how failing to do so is an example of epistemic injustice.

6. Epistemic Injustice and Language

In previous chapters, I talked about specific models and conceptions of autism. I also discussed the impact of specific approaches on the ethics of autism. For example, it is entirely different to consider autism primarily as a deficit of Theory of Mind and social functioning, rather than attributing the social challenges of autistic people to an overload of sensory experience. Thinking about autism as primarily a genetic condition is different from stating that the characteristics of someone we would consider autistic are only a dysfunction because Western society has narrowed our concept of normality. If we look at autism purely through a biomedical lens, we may consider it to be an individual's problem that needs to be detected and solved early. If we look at autism through the lens of Crip Theory, we notice that many stories are possible about people with a diagnosis. These stories do not eliminate one another but supplement and challenge each other. The neurodiversity movement gives people a voice and states that autism does not have to be a disorder at all. It can be part of someone's identity that does not need to be cured or prevented. The neurodiversity movement is a reaction to the often primarily medical discourse of many parents and autism professionals. It demonstrates that it is essential that many behaviours that we might consider as disruptive, non-adaptive or meaningless have a meaning for the autistic person

Testimony from autistic people can give us a lot of sensitive information. Think about the significance of certain stims. Stims are repetitive movements, such as flapping one's hands. Autistic people often describe these as a way to deal with stressful situations. They also explain why they have difficulty looking other people in the eyes: they experience eye contact as very intrusive. Such an explanation is

 https://doi.org/10.11647/OBP.0261.06

entirely different from stating that autistic people do not understand that eyes are the windows to the soul, as has sometimes been suggested. Nevertheless, autism researchers have long neglected such evidence. In this chapter, I discuss why it took a long time before people considered it to be valuable information. I analyse this as an example of epistemic injustice. I will also elaborate on what it means to incorporate the experiences of those who cannot express themselves very well in words, such as autistic people who do not use verbal language or people with an intellectual disability. I will argue that this does not mean that this testimony should be valued less, but that it is the moral duty of researchers, clinicians, and ethicists to actively search for ways to take seriously evidence that is harder to understand or collect.

A Sense of Self

In chapter three, I discussed what autistic persons often describe as one of the most important or challenging characteristics of autism: a different way of perceiving the world in sensory terms. Noises can be experienced as very loud, and smells can be overwhelming and sometimes even sickening. Some autistic people experience pain less frequently than people without autism. Such different sensory experiences have only been taken up in DSM-5 as diagnostic criteria since 2013.[1] How is it possible that this has been neglected for so long by autism researchers? To explain this, we can perhaps look at explanations given by some autism researchers themselves. One of the big names in the autism world, Uta Frith, describes in her book *Autism: Explaining the Enigma* how autistic people have a deficient sense of self and insight into their own self. [2] She makes a distinction between the experiences themselves and being introspectively conscious of these experiences. Becoming conscious of an experience happens, in our brains, at a different moment than the experience itself. The experience itself is thus the first level, while becoming conscious of it is the second. According to this theory, autistic people probably experience the same levels of pain, and hear

---

1   American Psychiatric Association, *Diagnostic and Statistical Manual of Mental Disorders (Fifth Ed.)* (Arlington: American Psychiatric Publishing, 2013).

2   Uta Frith, *Autism: Explaining the Enigma*, 2nd ed. (Malden, MA: Blackwell Pub, 2003).

or smell similarly to non-autistic people. However, they find it difficult to represent these experiences to themselves. Autistic people, because of their impaired sense of self, can misconstrue their own experiences. Hence, the argument goes, we should take the personal testimony of autistic people with a grain of salt. [3]

This idea has engendered many reactions. For example, Roberta Schriber and colleagues have found that, overall, autistic people have different personality types from non-autistic people, but their insights about their own personality are equally adequate.[4] A philosophical critique of the idea of a deficient insight in the autistic self comes from Victoria McGeer. In her article 'Autistic Self-Awareness', she gives different reasons why this way of thinking is wrong. She argues that autistic people, in their autobiographies, want to make sure that others understand them.[5] They understand that non-autistic people have different experiences and would like to share their own. Moreover, these autobiographies are often very precise and demonstrate that the authors want respect as people. This also sheds a different light on the problematic philosophical assumptions made by Utah Frith. The fact that autistic authors do talk clearly about their so-called misguided interpretation of their underlying perceptions and thoughts presupposes a third level on top of the levels of experience and perception of senses and thoughts, which would necessarily have to function well, as, at this level, the autistic person can talk clearly about their experiences, although the latter have been misinterpreted on the second level. McGeer states that it is perhaps better to assume that people who talk about their sensations do not talk about the perception of these sensations but the sensations themselves, an approach McGeer calls direct expressivist. If this is true, autistic accounts about sensations are precisely that: the expression of atypical sensations, rather than inaccurate expressions of typical sensations. We are best to take such accounts seriously.

3   Uta Frith and Francesca Happé, 'Theory of Mind and Self-Consciousness: What Is It Like to Be Autistic?', *Mind and Language*, 14:1 (1999), 1–22.

4   Roberta A. Schriber, Richard W. Robins, and Marjorie Solomon, 'Personality and Self-Insight in Individuals with Autism Spectrum Disorder', *Journal of Personality and Social Psychology*, 106:1 (2014), 112–30, https://doi.org/10.1037/a0034950

5   Victoria McGeer, 'Autistic Self-Awareness: Comment', *Philosophy, Psychiatry, and Psychology. Special Issue*, 11:3 (2004), 235–51.

Epistemic Injustice

Can a scientific theory that discredits the accounts of individual people be ethical? I think that not taking the stories of autistic people seriously is a form of epistemic injustice. This is a concept that Miranda Fricker develops in her book, *Epistemic Injustice*.[6] Epistemic injustice is the injustice that is inflicted on someone in their capacity as *someone who knows*. The person suffering epistemic injustice is not believed because they have a particular social identity.

An example is that many women will recognize that sometimes, when a woman proposes an idea in a meeting, this will be less readily acknowledged than when a man proposes the same idea later. Because we do not have reasons to assume that women propose less promising ideas, this is an injustice. Fricker distinguishes between two types of epistemic injustice: testimonial injustice and hermeneutic injustice. Testimonial injustice refers to the injustice done to an individual when others do not hear her testimony because she has a social role associated with less credibility. Women and people of colour are examples singled out by Fricker, but autistic autobiographers can also be victims of testimonial injustice if we assume that the autobiography cannot be a truthful representation of authentic experiences. That such injustice is dangerous goes without saying. Not only is it fundamentally unjust, but the victims also risk seeing themselves as someone who has less of a right to speak.

Fricker also describes a more structural form of epistemic injustice, hermeneutic injustice. She describes this as: 'The injustice of having some significant area of one's social experience obscured from collective understanding owing to structural identity prejudice in the collective hermeneutical resource.'[7] In her book, she gives an example of a woman in the mid-twentieth century who systematically suffered from sexual intimidation by her boss. Because experiences of such intimidation were not systematically shared, as people did not take women seriously, women felt alone with their experiences. Thus, hermeneutic injustice means that specific experiences of suppressed groups are not available

---

6   Miranda Fricker, *Epistemic Injustice: Power and the Ethics of Knowing* (Oxford: Clarendon Press, 2007).

7   Fricker, *Epistemic Injustice*, p. 155.

in the public domain as an expression of social injustice. This can lead to human beings who belong to this group considering their own experiences as unimportant and marginal.

Moreover, as some of these experiences are crucial for one's own identity, hermeneutic injustice could lead to individual human beings being unable to develop themselves fully and be who they are or want to be. This form of epistemic injustice seems to apply to autism; for example, if the experiences of autistic people are not part of scientific research into autism. Considering the existence of the neurodiversity movement and the growing corpus of 'auti-biographies', this seems to be changing: autistic people are able to define what it is to experience autism more than they were before. It is essential to consider these experiences in research and clinical practice too. Moreover, we must not only consider one version of autistic experience. If we only consider the experiences of those with whom we share a common verbal language, we also do an injustice.

We could also ask ourselves whether the fact that autism as a diagnosis only became generally accessible to adults in recent decades is not an injustice in itself. I described in chapter four how autism as a named phenomenon only recently came about. This is perhaps because, previously, the challenges that autistic people experienced were not perceived as salient, so there was no need to name it. In this respect, speculation that historical figures such as the philosopher Jeremy Bentham may have been autistic make no sense.[8] We cannot know for sure whether Bentham suffered from the fact that he was eccentric. Perhaps he lived in an environment in which that was not, by definition, a drawback. It could also be the case that these historical figures felt that they were different and felt alone in their difference. The fact that in the past — and perhaps also in the present, in countries where a diagnosis is not widely available — shared experiences of being autistic were not available could be considered as hermeneutic injustice.

We can look from two different perspectives at the post-factum diagnosis of historical figures. If the peculiarities and behaviour of, for example, Jeremy Bentham were not problematic in his time and did not cause him suffering, they probably did not need a name. This view

---

8   Philip Lucas and Anne Sheeran, 'Asperger's Syndrome and the Eccentricity and
      Genius of Jeremy Bentham', *Journal of Bentham Studies*, 8 (2006), 1–37.

corresponds to the idea of autism as a clinical diagnosis, a phenomenon that requires intervention and support. Nevertheless, this does not take away from the fact that Bentham and others could have had specific characteristics associated with autism. However, at that time, this was not sufficient to be considered a psychiatric condition. Let us assume that Bentham was aware that he was somewhat atypical and that this caused him suffering. We could state that the absence of the diagnostic category of autism, or even the lack of acknowledgement that certain people are different and should receive support for their specific difference, is a kind of hermeneutic injustice. Fricker herself might call this bad luck: the science about autism that would allow the creation of shared stories was simply not available. Nevertheless, the difference between bad luck and injustice is difficult to draw post factum. When looking at the examples Fricker gives that relate to women, we could play devil's advocate and suggest that the science to say that women are equally valid human beings just was not there. Fricker states that there has to be social injustice, as in the case of oppressed women, in order to be able to talk about hermeneutic injustice. In the case of the diagnosis of historical figures, it is difficult to know whether social injustice was at play and whether Bentham suffered from the fact that he may have been considered unusual or peculiar by his community.

We arrive here at the fundamental question of who can say something about autism. I have no diagnosis, and although there are more and more autistic autism researchers, they are still a minority. Can I, as a non-diagnosed researcher, say something meaningful about the ethics of autism? Is that in itself not a form of normative violence? If we would oppose feminist ethics that are solely devised by men, perhaps we should have the same reservations about autistic ethics developed by people without a diagnosis. I do not have a straightforward answer to this question, and I feel some discomfort about it. I think it is essential to research autism in a spirit of openness towards, and with input from the autistic community. Autistic researchers are often an essential source of information about autism. This can take the form of an autoethnography, such as in the paper 'Aut-ors of our Experience' by Jessica Benham and James Kizer. This essay is a somewhat subversive but simultaneously clarifying and direct source of information.[9] The authors, academics with

9   Jessica L. Benham and James S. Kizer, 'Aut-ors of Our Experience: Interrogating Intersections of Autistic Identity', *Canadian Journal of Disability Studies*, 5:3 (2016), 77–113.

an autism diagnosis, talk about their experiences as autistic researchers and lecturers in short fragments. A recurrent theme is their attempts to pass as 'normal', while at the same time recognising that this was not wholly possible and also perhaps not desirable. It struck me that their experiences as junior lecturers, together with all the insecurities attached to this, was also readily recognizable, even for someone without a diagnosis. In their text, the authors explicitly aim to be disruptive: with the fragmentary layout of the text, using different fonts, they want to create a jarring experience for the reader. In this way, they want to relay the particular and different nature of the autistic experience. My students wondered whether this actually conveyed the message better or whether it would scare readers away. However, such a disruptive approach makes sense, especially if we keep in mind that non-autistic researchers write the vast majority of literature about autism.

Language and Autism

There is something particular to each experience, autistic or not, and although autistic researchers may be better suited to represent autistic experiences correctly, these findings cannot be generalized either. Many autistic people do not use verbal language, for example, but we do need to devise methods to incorporate the experiences of those who do not do so or who have cognitive challenges. Scientific research is primarily language-based, and even research that puts the experiences of autistic people at the centre will often be based on spoken or written communication. Nevertheless, autism is also associated with challenges in communication and language.

The following paragraphs are based on a talk I gave about autism and multilingualism in autumn 2017 in the Dutch town of Sittard. Based on my research into the experiences of adults with an autism diagnosis, I discussed the relationship between autism and language. On the one hand, spoken language is the most prevalent means of communication. However, this is often not how an autistic person prefers to communicate. Communication should be shared between autistic people and non-autistic people, and we should strive to come to a common method of communicating. I applied my ideas to the question of what multilingualism means for autistic people as an illustration:

what can we learn from autistic people themselves, and what does this imply for learning and speaking different languages?

Autism and language have been linked from autism's conceptualisation as a child psychiatric disorder onwards—the earliest diagnostic instruments mentioned communication challenges. Kanner's original article describes several children that either used minimal language or used language in a particular way: they changed pronouns. They often repeated words that were said by others, a phenomenon called echolalia. For a long time, diagnosticians distinguished between Asperger syndrome and classic autism by using mastery of language. People with Asperger syndrome have typical language development, although they may experience challenges in understanding what someone intends. People with 'classic autism' develop language late or never. The DSM-5 gathers all these phenomena under the name Autism Spectrum Disorder (ASD), and communication challenges can become apparent in different ways. A new classification has also been added: Social (Pragmatic) Communication Disorder (SCD), which includes the social challenges that define ASD, but without the second criterion (limited and repetitive patterns of behaviour and interests and activities). It is a diagnosis that can be made after ASD has been ruled out.

Nevertheless, diagnostic criteria are elaborated in observations of behaviour. Autism is diagnosed based on these observations and on the assessment of whether the behaviour leads to certain problems. According to Laurent Mottron, an autism expert from Canada, there is a link between the specific intelligence of autistic children, who, according to him, have strong visual intelligence, and their use of language.[10] He points out that many autistic children are hyperlexic: their interests in images and written language occur before their interest in oral language.

To better understand how autistic people experience the world, I have interviewed adults with a diagnosis of autism together with Raymond Langenberg, who himself has a diagnosis of Asperger syndrome. Because some people with autism are not comfortable using spoken language, we asked our respondents whether they would like to do these interviews via chat, email or live. We talked about the following:

---

10   Laurent Mottron, *L'intervention précoce pour enfants autistes: Nouveaux principes pour soutenir une autre intelligence* (Brussels: Editions Mardaga, 2016).

feeling different and the suffering that sensory overload sometimes causes, the importance of language, and the feeling of having one's own way of communicating that is not understood or appreciated by others. For example, one participant, Nora, describes how she had communicated with another autistic person via cards and images rather than words. She experienced this way of communicating as much more expressive than merely using spoken words. Nora loves to dance, and dancing allows her to express her deepest feelings. Another respondent, Bas, has found that ways of expressing himself that differ from standard verbal communication are not considered fully valid by therapists. Bas is a musician; he has played music since he was a child and he only plays his own compositions. He also ran a music shop for a while. Music is a natural way for him to express himself, but therapists attributed to him a 'minimal inner world' because he could not express that inner world very well in standard language.

In the video *In My Language* (2007), Mel Baggs (1980–2020) shows strikingly how verbal communication is not the only way to relate to reality.[11] Baggs had been diagnosed with low-functioning autism' because she did not speak. Via the video, she questions what it means to be 'low-functioning'. She shows her own language: a more direct way of dealing with reality by humming and feeling. Her method of communicating was not lesser, but different. That human beings are linguistic beings is frequently stated. Often, we automatically assume that others use oral language. However, through our interviews, I wondered why other ways of expression would not be equally valid. We might consider the other means of expression by autistic people as a different language, such as Baggs explicitly did by referring to her 'own language'.

Nevertheless, communication is always mutual. People who prefer a language that most people do not share, either because they speak a different language or prefer a different way of expressing themselves, have a disadvantage. If we consider language in an extended sense, perhaps autistic children and adults have always been bilingual. During my interviews, something that also struck me is that these autistic adults often wanted to write about their experiences: they kept diaries,

---

11   Mel Baggs, *In My Language* (2007), https://www.youtube.com/watch?v=JnylM1 hI2jc

wrote books, and documented their experiences. There was a great wish to communicate, although not always in the standard way. Autibiographies also demonstrate a different way of being in the world, albeit one that can be communicated. Somewhere in the middle, it must be possible for typical and less typical people to relate to one another.

What does this mean for multilingualism and autism, the subject of the conference at which I gave this presentation? Some autism professionals argue that autistic children may be overburdened by learning another language because they already experience challenges with their mother tongue. Research has demonstrated that there is no proof that this is so: autistic children can be fluent in multiple languages. At the same time, being able to speak multiple languages might improve their executive functioning. [12] It may be the case that autistic adults have always been multilingual in a certain sense. The methods of communicating they prefer are perhaps different from the preferences of their close contacts. They have to translate their natural way of dealing with communication into something more standard. It would be interesting to learn more about what this means for the acquisition of an additional language.

Of course, autism is a heterogeneous phenomenon. There is probably something atypical in the autistic use of language, as this is one of the diagnostic criteria for autism. However, this is hard to pin down to one single cause or to one single way of expression. Laurent Mottron, who is perhaps overly restrictive in applying the term autism to a specific conception of autism—that of visual intelligence—states that we should not force autistic children into using common means of communication. Instead, we should work with their interests and ways of expressing themselves. We can use this approach to communicate with children who do not talk but are interested in reading and visual images from an early age.

Nevertheless, it remains the case that this atypical communication also makes people vulnerable: you become vulnerable if you are unable to express yourself in the same way as the majority, and consequently it is often necessary to have a common language and learn a more widely-used method of communicating. However, if we want to understand the

---

12   Ana Maria Gonzalez-Barrero and Aparna S. Nadig, 'Can Bilingualism Mitigate Set-Shifting Difficulties in Children With Autism Spectrum Disorders?', *Child Development*, 2017, https://doi.org/10.1111/cdev.12979

relationship between language acquisition, communication preference, and autism better, we should probably first gain insight into what it means for autistic people to experience language differently. Together with them, we should look for alternative communication methods if they are uncomfortable with spoken language, and come to a mutual understanding. Although we may be expecting too much from autistic children if we ask them to learn yet another language, it may be an opportunity.

An example of this approach can be found in the movie *Life, Animated* (2016), in which the parents of the autistic main character discover that they can communicate with their son via the dialogue of Disney characters, and, in this way, share a common language. Perhaps some children are very visual thinkers, or like to learn many different languages. There is perhaps no readily available answer to the question of whether multilingualism and autism go well together. We must learn from the child herself. Is she a visual thinker, and what are her interests? What is her preferred way of communication? What can we learn from her?

In this chapter, I have described how not taking the experiences and testimony of autistic people seriously can be considered epistemic injustice. This is relevant to ethics research, but I would contend it is also important for scientific research. Research that tries to explain a behavioural phenomenon linked to a specific experience of the world would do well to incorporate an understanding of this experience. Granted, this may be complicated because some autistic people may have different communication preferences or not use verbal language at all. Nonetheless, this does not make research into people's experiences less important. It only means that we may have to try harder. In the next chapter, I will put this conclusion into practice and present some of the research that Raymond Langenberg and I did with adults who had received a recent diagnosis of autism.

7. Experiences of Autism

(written with Raymond Langenberg)

It is a form of epistemic injustice to not engage with the experiences of autistic people in scientific research and ethical reflection. A book that claims to research the conditions of possibility of an ethics of autism should pay attention to these experiences. In the last years, the research into autistic experiences has taken a significant leap forward.[1] Autistic researchers wrote books about their own experiences and that of other autistic adults.[2] For example, the book *Aquamarine Blue 5* describes the experience of autistic students at university.[3] There are more and more initiatives in different countries that enable autistic people to have a say in agenda-setting research, such as PARC (Participatory Autism Research Collective) in the United Kingdom and LAVA (Lees-en Adviesgroep Volwassenen met Autisme), a Belgian initiative of autistic people who share input, advice, and priorities with Belgian autism researchers.

What follows is a reflection of my study into adults' experiences with a diagnosis of autism. I conducted this study with Raymond Langenberg, who was diagnosed with Asperger syndrome fifteen years ago. We interviewed twenty-two adults. One of them decided to withdraw from the study for personal reasons. We got approval for the study from the ethics committee of the University of Antwerp, the ethische adviescommissie voor sociale en humane wetenschappen (EA

---

1   Jaci C. Huws, and Robert S. P. Jones, 'Diagnosis, Disclosure, and Having Autism: An Interpretative Phenomenological Analysis of the Perceptions of Young People with Autism', *Journal of Intellectual & Developmental Disability*, 33 (2008), 99–107.

2   Damian Milton, *A Mismatch of Salience: Explorations of the Nature of Autism from Theory to Practice* (London: Pavillion, 2017).

3   Dawn Prince-Hughes, *Aquamarine Blue 5: Personal Stories of College Students with Autism* (Athens: Ohio University Press, 2002).

 https://doi.org/10.11647/OBP.0261.07

SHW). Participants signed a form to demonstrate informed consent and chose a pseudonym that we used in the reports. For our research, we chose to use Interpretative Phenomenological Analysis as the approach.[4] This method is characterized by an emphasis on idiography, describing and appreciating particular cases and experiences, and on a double hermeneutics: participants themselves give meaning to their experiences. Researchers interpret this attribution of meaning. This meant that participants could read their quotes and our interpretation of these quotes and comment on them. We recruited via the Vlaamse Vereniging voor Autisme and on social media such as Facebook and Twitter. Two participants were personal acquaintances of the authors. In order to consider the stories in as unbiased a manner as possible, we did not ask to look at the participants' diagnostic reports, nor did we want to know their IQ. All had an official diagnosis given at a diagnostic centre. Participants could choose from an oral interview, a chat session or an email conversation. Some requested to look at the interview guide in advance because they would like to know what they would be asked. Our respondents shared with us their life trajectories before the diagnosis, as well as the diagnostic process itself, and life after the diagnosis.

After the interviews, we first did an inductive analysis of the themes. We did not use any software, but we noted themes separately in the margins of the transcript. We met every two weeks to check our findings and uncover common categories. In a later phase, we laid down the story of our book. *Experiences of Adults Following an Autism Diagnosis* is a descriptive text subdivided into seven broader themes.[5] Another text, which was published in 2017 as a separate chapter in a volume on citizenship, contains a summary of the research.[6] We presented the research findings at four different conferences and we took suggestions into account during the interpretation of our findings. In what follows, I present a couple of quotes and their interpretations. They demonstrate

---

4   Jonathan Smith, *Interpretative Phenomenological Analysis: Theory, Method and Research*, 1st edition (Los Angeles: SAGE Publications Ltd, 2009).

5   Kristien Hens and Raymond Langenberg, *Experiences of Adults Following an Autism Diagnosis* (Cham: Palgrave Macmillan, 2018).

6   Kristien Hens and Raymond Langenberg, 'Immeasurability, Biology, Identity. Citizenship and the Meaning of a Diagnostic Label for Adults Diagnosed with Autism', in *Citizenship in Organizations. Practicing the Immeasurable.*, ed. by Suzan Langenberg and Fleur Beyers (London: Palgrave Macmillan, 2017), pp. 201–23.

how autism is not solely a static 'given' in the life of the individual, but instead how the meaning of autism and the diagnosis of autism changes throughout the individual's life. This discussion functions as an introduction to the final part of this book, which presents dynamic conceptions of autism.

Although autism has been initially conceived of as a childhood disorder, more and more adults receive the diagnosis. This is challenging in different ways. Firstly, to qualify for a diagnosis, the individual should be hampered in their everyday functioning, to such an extent that this poses insurmountable problems in their social or professional life. We could explain the fact that this person did not receive the diagnosis as a child or adolescent by stating that they were not dysfunctional at that moment, that they received a faulty diagnosis, or that their dysfunctioning was not obvious enough. Nevertheless, as soon as the diagnosis of autism is attributed, this implies that the condition has existed since birth. Secondly, clinicians consider diagnosis challenging in adults because they have learned to cope with their autism through a range of masking strategies.[7] Therefore some suggest that autism is a lifelong condition, but it is visible or invisible depending on whether and how the individual can adapt. The question then arises: how does this relate to the idea that autism is a diagnosis given if there is evidence of dysfunctioning? Indeed, the case of adults without an intellectual disability who receive a diagnosis of autism implies a more dynamic understanding of autism. An understanding that explains dysfunctioning based on a specific vulnerability (whether it is genetic, neurological, or cognitive) in interaction with environmental and social factors seems adequate. Below, I describe confrontations with and learning from others. Such feedback is, in the first place, given by people with whom our participants interacted. It is also a mechanism of the diagnosis itself, a label that can be assimilated, rejected, or transcended.

Autism, as defined in DSM-5, is characterized by 'social and communicative problems'. Furthermore, our respondents described how they felt that their challenges were often linked to misunderstanding

---

7   Iliana Magiati, 'Assessment in Adulthood', in *Handbook of Assessment and Diagnosis of Autism Spectrum Disorder*, ed. by Johnny L. Matson, Autism and Child Psychopathology Series (New York: Springer International Publishing, 2016), pp. 191–207, https://doi.org/10.1007/978-3-319-27171-2_11

others or not being understood by others. This could happen, for example, because they took the words of others literally or could not detect deception. Baukis, who was sixty at the time of the interview and who had recently received her diagnosis, described how she was sexually abused on different occasions:

> When I was between sixteen and twenty-six years of age, many things went wrong, specifically in the relationship with boys. It was a disaster. I was very gullible. I was a toy for many people. I was raped a couple of times because I did not understand the world.
>
> On the one hand, I had an enormous need for connection. That is the thread in my life, and I think that is so for most people. But how do you do that without making yourself vulnerable, without being hurt?

Baukis' story, and specifically this quote, is illuminating for different reasons. Like many of our participants, she describes a heartfelt desire for connection with others. However, she is easily deceived into thinking that others have good intentions. For Baukis, these moments of deception and even abuse were not instructive. On the contrary, even if a simplistic reading of autism (as the inability to read the intentions of others) seems applicable here, the question remains where the problem lies: in the person who is gullible and looks for genuine connection, or in those who can 'read' such a vulnerability and abuse it? Baukis explains how her diagnosis has helped her to understand that she has experienced many challenges in her life.

Hanna, thirty-five, describes how the reactions of others have pushed her towards trying to fit in:

> I was acutely aware that I was always left out. I remember that, from the age of three, that specific behaviour made other people uncomfortable. That meant that I shouldn't do that anymore. And each time I thought, that is not allowed, I should do this, I should do that. Thus, you learn not to do things anymore. I have learned that I should not shout: leave me alone. And if you are bizarre or act strange, this is also not good.

The adverse reactions of others taught Hanna to adapt. Although she does not suggest, at least in this quote, that this is something negative, it is evident in this interview and others that such compensating behaviour does help her to function better in society. However, it is at the same time felt as a loss of who one is. Moreover, it left participants with feelings of fatigue. Indeed, they often gave voice to the sense that they could never be genuinely themselves, to the extent that, in the end, they did not know who they really were because of the strategies of compensation and camouflage they had taught themselves.

Others are often valuable sources of information, feedback, and opportunities to develop and learn. Karel was fifty-five when he was interviewed, and he had received his diagnosis of Asperger syndrome fifteen years before. In this study, he is the one who lived with his diagnosis the longest. He explained how he was somewhat isolated as a child and grew up in an environment that did not encourage him to break out of his isolation. Nevertheless, he says:

> I think you can call it a kind of hunger, a feeling that I needed more than my own understanding of what was available in my direct environment. But on my own I was not able to open myself up.

Rather than an unwillingness to connect with others, or a lack of interest in such human contact, Karel experienced a desire for more that remained unsatisfied. He continues:

> I was too isolated; I was too concerned about myself and got stuck. I could be very childish and provoke people, but I could not think about myself in these terms. So I confronted many people and tried to get in touch with them.

As a teenager, Karel wanted to learn more about himself and how to function in the world. He knew that he could only learn by communication and in relation to others. He felt, however, growing up in an environment that did not afford him many responses from others, that he did not receive the necessary feedback. He tells how he was sometimes so isolated that he got lost in his thoughts:

> There were periods that I thought that I was not entirely there. I was semi-conscious. I was not entirely there, you know. I have it now, and I had it as a child. I can do things for hours or be immersed in something, but really deeply immersed. Does that mean I am different from others? You can only know that if someone talks to you or if you are in contact with the other.

You can only know if certain feelings of being *apart from your environment* are normal — or if you are different in some respects — when you are in contact with others who share or do not share similar experiences.

These others, whether they are friends or family, can also function as a touchstone. For example, Robyn, thirty, talks about how she was looking for a new job. She tells how her friends gave her feedback about what kind of job would be suitable for her. She says she had three job offers, and she had managed to choose 'the worst of all three', against the advice of her friends:

> I had a choice between two different jobs, and everyone told me to take one specific, and I completely did not understand why. So finally they tried very hard their best to explain this to me, and then I understood. But I had managed to choose the job from all three with the lowest wages, the most stressful, farthest from home and with the vaguest job description.

She chose this job because the job title sounded interesting and the deal included a company car. She continues: 'I notice that that happens to me a lot, that I have to check twice with people because otherwise, I have a completely different and wrong idea of what something really is.' Even if Robyn admits that she probably made a mistake in choosing that job, she does understand, after consultation with her friends, why that was the case. She learns how to understand her own choices better and how to translate this into future decision-making.

Interview participants explained how they used input from others and confrontations with others to understand themselves and others better. For participants in a relationship, their partner often gave necessary feedback without wanting to change them. Some of our participants counted on friends. Those who had a joyous childhood stressed that their parents had understood their ways of being, and so they could grow into adults without at that point requiring a diagnosis.

At a certain point in their adult lives, all our respondents encountered specific challenges that proved to be insurmountable without professional help. In many cases, they took the initiative to ask for a diagnostic examination that eventually led to a diagnosis of autism or Asperger syndrome. With this diagnosis, a different kind of confrontation happened. They were confronted with the implications of the test results on the one hand, and with societal expectations about the meaning of such a diagnosis on the other. Our participants' reaction varied from an almost complete acceptance of the diagnosis to a rejection of the many associations of autism.

On the one hand, they accepted autism as an accurate description of their functioning. Some participants had previously received a diagnosis of personality disorder — such as Borderline Personality Disorder — and could relate much better to autism. On the other hand, our respondents stated that they did not entirely fit the stereotypical image of an autistic person. Many also contradicted the idea that autistic people are 'loners' or lack empathy. Nevertheless, overall our respondents did recognize themselves in a description of 'autism'.

Receiving a diagnosis and informing others about it changes one's relationship with these others. The official diagnosis is, for many participants, a way to explain one's particularities. Expectations become adjusted, and problems that would previously lead to conflict are now readily explained because of the diagnosis. Thus, Hanna states:

> What is really nice, I have a really good bond with my parents, but we had always had so many conflicts in the past. [...] Since they know about my diagnosis, this is no longer so. They have found a different way to approach me, and I really appreciate that. Before, they would confront me and say, oh, Hanna, you shouldn't do that, try to be a bit less black and white. And now they say, we know that we won't let it explode, we tackle it, it is OK.

The diagnosis itself can also engender new expectations from others. What autism is, besides the stereotypes and in the specific context of a person, remains hard to grasp. Sandra (thirty-eight at the time of the interview) suffers from sensory hypersensitivity. Although she appreciates the insight offered by the diagnosis, she regrets that other people, especially in a professional context, conclude that she functions better in a job without contact with clients:

> At the moment the diagnosis was given, I received a different job. I am now seated at a different desk; it is a desk without colleagues. It is a bit lonely. I know this works best for me, but sometimes they exaggerate. I know it is to protect me, but I do not think that I am a danger to other people.

Although, in her previous job, she suffered from extreme fatigue, Sandra thinks that sitting alone in a separate room is better in some ways, but on the other hand, it is lonely. In other parts of the interview, she stresses that the extra compensations she gets at work through her diagnosis are based on a general feeling about what autism is rather than what it means specifically for her.

A formal diagnosis not only changes the relationship one has with others, but also how one understands oneself. The diagnosis is an external evaluation that influences one's self-image. It is true that some of our respondents automatically recognized themselves in their diagnosis, but they also each had to find out what the diagnosis meant for them. Karel explains this as follows:

> It offers an insight that can inspire, that can help you reorient yourself. But you still have to make it your own so that you can build it into your own actions. For example, now I can accept that I may sometimes go into too much detail. But that is again simplifying it. A diagnosis offers focal points, which you can research. How does this fit into my own pattern of actions? It is an extra critical factor that can be confronting or can offer peace of mind and a way to think about it. That was not explained to me when I received my diagnosis because the world of diagnoses is hyper flat.

Hence a diagnosis can offer self-insight, but only after the person diagnosed comes to terms with it and integrates it in their self-image. This process is something that many adults we interviewed went through without external help. Some did receive therapy, but that therapy was often not aimed at the development of such self-insight. Another participant, BartDelam, explained how the insight given by the diagnosis helped him surpass the limitations of that diagnosis. He uses the example of how, before receiving the diagnosis, he became outraged when children were playing noisily in a playground close to his house because he is susceptible to noise. The diagnosis offered him insight into these emotions and allowed him to deal with them better:

> Before the diagnosis, I would probably have been someone who would file a complaint about the noise if there had been a playground behind the house. Now I try to think, what can I do about it, put on headphones... Children play and make noise. Of course, looking at it differently does not help a lot because the noise is still there.

It is important to note that the diagnosis could have given him an extra reason to be even angrier. It is an acknowledgement that he experiences certain sounds more intensely than other people. Instead, the narrative provided by the diagnosis offered him an opportunity to look at his functioning critically, from a distance.

Autism is considered a neurodevelopmental disorder present very early in life and persisting throughout the lifespan. Although many participants have experienced challenges in their lives and have felt different from others as a result, our study demonstrates that we cannot interpret their stories in a unidimensional and straightforward way. Perhaps they show how a vulnerability that might be neurological can lead to challenges later in life, and how these people have dealt with this vulnerability in their interaction with others. We suspect that there may indeed be a genetic or innate predisposition towards an atypical cognitive or social development that is not always translated into problems. Still, it is very enlightening to learn how people have dealt with their problems before and after the diagnosis. This suggests that an approach that exclusively targets problems and challenges within individuals is problematic and often futile.

Qualitative research that is geared at investigating lived experiences and evaluating how people interpret their own experiences is also relevant to judge the appropriateness of specific explanatory models. For example, in the year 2000, Robert Jones, Andrew Zahl, and Jaci Huws used the first-person narratives of autistic people to demonstrate that — contrary to prevailing theories — autistic people have strong emotions.[8] David Trembath and colleagues used focus groups to research how young adults diagnosed with autism experience feelings of fear: what are the occasions for this, the consequences of it, and which solutions do these young people use to deal with it?[9] Our respondents have demonstrated that they interact dynamically with others to build their own stories. Confrontation and contact with others can be a source of suffering but also a learning opportunity.

We gave an example of how challenges with interaction can lead to deception and even abuse. Such challenges are not (only) related to a difficulty within the autistic person him- or herself. Abuse is the result of

8   Robert S. P. Jones, Andrew Zahl, and Jaci C. Huws, 'First-Hand Accounts of Emotional Experiences in Autism: A Qualitative Analysis', *Disability & Society*, 16:3 (2001), 393–401, https://doi.org/10.1080/09687590120045950

9   David Trembath and others, 'The Experience of Anxiety in Young Adults With Autism Spectrum Disorders', *Focus on Autism and Other Developmental Disabilities*, 27:4 (2012), 213–24, https://doi.org/10.1177/1088357612454916

deception by another. Trying to conform to social expectations can also lead to interactions going awry, as this involves 'giving something up' to 'belong'. Sarah Bargiela and her colleagues described these mechanisms in fourteen women who received their diagnoses when they were adults. They described how nine out of the fourteen women experienced a form of abuse, and felt that they applied a masking strategy and camouflaged themselves in order to belong to a group. The authors describe how the diagnosis gave these women a way to create a narrative within which their differences and communication styles could fit, and how this eased communication.[10]

Laura Hannah and Steven Stagg described negative sexual experiences following an abuse of trust.[11] Besides these breaches of trust to which autistic persons, often women, are subjected, social interaction can also become a learning opportunity. Our respondents expressed a genuine desire to learn from others and improve their social interactions. This is in line with the findings of Fleur Wiorkowski, who interviewed twelve participants who had a diagnosis of autism about their experiences during higher education. She found that her respondents enjoyed social interaction, mostly when they met people with similar interests. This enabled them to learn from their interactions. She explains that, although we may expect group assignments to be less than ideal for students with this diagnosis, her participants stated that they saw it as an opportunity to learn.[12]

In this and other research into the experiences of autistic people, it becomes apparent that autism is not solely a fixed identity that is persistent throughout one's life. We have described how the diagnosis is a description of one's functioning and can form the basis of how others understand you. As such, it is often a welcome explanation of the challenges that people with autism experience. Nonetheless, the

---

10 Sarah Bargiela, Robyn Steward, and William Mandy, 'The Experiences of Late-Diagnosed Women with Autism Spectrum Conditions: An Investigation of the Female Autism Phenotype', *Journal of Autism and Developmental Disorders*, 46:10 (2016), 3281–94, https://doi.org/10.1007/s10803-016-2872-8

11 Laura A. Hannah and Steven D. Stagg, 'Experiences of Sex Education and Sexual Awareness in Young Adults with Autism Spectrum Disorder', *Journal of Autism and Developmental Disorders*, 46:12 (2016), 3678–87, https://doi.org/10.1007/s10803-016-2906-2

12 Fleur Wiorkowski, 'The Experiences of Students with Autism Spectrum Disorders in College: A Heuristic Exploration', *The Qualitative Report*, 20:6 (2015), 847.

meaning of autism and of the diagnosis of autism changes. There are possibilities for learning and misunderstanding in interactions with others, and even when answering the question of what it means to be autistic. In the last part of the book, I will suggest how we can conceive of autism as a biologically real yet dynamic phenomenon. But firstly the next chapter, an interlude, will offer some speculative reflections on autism and time.

8. Interlude

Autism and Time

Until now, I have talked about the different meanings of autism and about the importance of incorporating stories of people's experiences into the study of autism. In what follows, I will give the account of a talk that I gave in 2017 at a symposium on time, organized by Hipposocrates, a Flemish organization of medicine and philosophy. I write this as an interlude: those readers who would like to skip its more speculative content may do so without losing this book's main thread.

The idea for the talk arose from a fascination that I had had for some time: the experience of time and the handling of time by autistic people. It may look as though I am falling into the same trap I have been warning about: that I take a particular consequence of autism, that of experiencing time differently, as absolute. That is not at all the intention. A different perception of time is something that autistic people often talk about when talking about their own experiences. Therefore it makes sense to say something about time and autism without assuming that this is the same experience for all autistic people, or that a changed perception of time is the ultimate explanatory model of autism. Moreover, time is, just like autism, a layered and complex concept. It is not my idea here to tell a consistent story about time itself, but perhaps I can say something about the relevance of time for the philosophy and ethics of autism.

It is helpful to start this account with an acknowledgement that there is no simple answer to the question of what time is. For example, the space-time concept of the physicist, for example, Albert Einstein's theory of relativity, whether it is the special or general variant, is not very useful when we think about the challenges of a sense of time. We can even wonder whether there is such a thing as the past, present, and future.

  https://doi.org/10.11647/OBP.0261.08

Perhaps there is only a simultaneity — a point on the axis from which one has an experience of (linear) time.[1] Alternatively, maybe it is the case, as Belgian chemist Ilya Prigogine suggests, that the irreversibility of time is foundational for our reality. In what follows, we shall consider the experience of time rather than a correct definition of time.

In one way or another, at least according to evolutionary psychologists, our 'neurological wiring' evolved to experience time the way we do now: as past, present, and future. We name occurrences in our universe in an orderly manner. We experience time as progressive: after the sun, there is rain. After summer comes autumn. We live on a planet with a circadian rhythm, and perhaps, therefore, evolution has taken care that this rhythm is the basis of our sense of time. Time is also linked with our biology. Indeed, it seems to be the case that the smaller an animal is, or the briefer the time it lives, the slower it experiences time. For a fly, it seems, time goes by very slowly. Moreover, that is useful to her, because if you tried to kill her, she sees your hand moving very slowly, and she can fly away before you can blink an eye. Perhaps we might even say that the past-present-future complex is a mere construction of our brain.[2] If so, the 'now' is all present sensory impressions, and the past is the most relevant of these in the banks of our memory, and the future is that which we can imagine but not predict definitely. In any case, it is essential to realize that a sense of time, like language, is also a shared experience.[3] If time turns out to be an illusion, it is at least a shared illusion, one in which we are, to some extent, synchronized. It would be difficult to live in a community with others in which everyone had their own idiosyncratic sense of time. It would be challenging to maintain a discussion with a fly.

I have already extensively discussed the question of what autism is. In one sense, autism is a diagnostic category, or — to put it more succinctly — a diagnosis. Since 2013, and the advent of DSM-5, you are

---

1   Thomas Fuchs and Zeno Van Duppen, 'Time and Events: On the Phenomenology of Temporal Experience in Schizophrenia (Ancillary Article to EAWE Domain 2)', *Psychopathology*, 50:1 (2017), 68–74, https://doi.org/10.1159/000452768

2   Camilo R. Gomez, 'Time Is Brain: The Stroke Theory of Relativity', *Journal of Stroke and Cerebrovascular Diseases: The Official Journal of National Stroke Association*, 2018, https://doi.org/10.1016/j.jstrokecerebrovasdis.2018.04.001

3   Lera Boroditsky, 'How Languages Construct Time', in *Space, Time and Number in the Brain*, ed. by Stanislas Dehaene and Elizabeth Brannon (Oxford: Oxford University Press, 2011), pp. 333–41.

autistic if a psychiatrist, in collaboration with a multidisciplinary team, thinks that you have social or communicative problems, exhibit sufficient repetitive behaviours or restricted interests, and that these challenges affect your everyday life to a certain extent. A sense of time is not part of the diagnostic criteria. In chapter three, we saw how different theories explain why this cluster of behaviours that we call autism occur together. The most well-known explanatory model is that of a deficient Theory of Mind.[4] Besides that, there is the theory that autistic people have Weak Central Coherence.[5] Alternatively, they may experience difficulties with planning because of a problem with their executive functions.[6] More recent views are based on first-person experiences of autistic people and suggest that those with autism have a superior visual intelligence.[7] Some suggest that autistic people cannot filter out the stimuli of their senses sufficiently, so the world is too intense for them.[8] Other researchers have suggested that the predictive models by which our brain functions and allows us to experience the world efficiently do not work in a typical way in autistic people, who continuously see the world as it is, at great intensity.[9] Little is said about time in these models, although sometimes a link is made between, for example, an atypical sense of time and weak executive functioning, or a different way of dealing with predictions.[10]

If little is said (or known) about autism and sense of time, why dedicate an entire chapter to it? Based on stories by and about autistic

---

4   Simon Baron-Cohen, Alan M. Leslie, and Uta Frith, 'Does the Autistic Child Have a "Theory of Mind"?', *Cognition*, 21:1 (1985), 37–46.

5   Francesca Happé and Uta Frith, 'The Weak Coherence Account: Detail-Focused Cognitive Style in Autism Spectrum Disorders', *Journal of Autism and Developmental Disorders*, 36:1 (2006), 5–25, https://doi.org/10.1007/s10803-005-0039-0

6   James Russell, *Autism as an Executive Disorder* (Oxford: Oxford University Press, 1997).

7   Laurent Mottron and others, 'Enhanced Perceptual Functioning in Autism: An Update, and Eight Principles of Autistic Perception', *Journal of Autism and Developmental Disorders*, 36:1 (2006), 27–43, https://doi.org/10.1007/s10803-005-0040-7

8   Henry Markram, Tania Rinaldi, and Kamila Markram, 'The Intense World Syndrome — an Alternative Hypothesis for Autism', *Frontiers in Neuroscience*, 1:1 (2007), 77–96, https://doi.org/10.3389/neuro.01.1.1.006.2007

9   Sander Van de Cruys and others, 'Precise Minds in Uncertain Worlds: Predictive Coding in Autism', *Psychological Review*, 121:4 (2014), 649–75, https://doi.org/10.1037/a0037665

10   Pawan Sinha and others, 'Autism as a Disorder of Prediction', *Proceedings of the National Academy of Sciences*, 111:42 (2014), 15220–25, https://doi.org/10.1073/pnas.1416797111

people, there seems to be something atypical in the autistic sense of time. To grasp what this could be, I will give some examples from fiction and from my research.[11] My first example is *Martian Time-Slip*, a novel from 1964 by Philip K. Dick.[12] The story deals with a colony on Mars and is an allegory of the colonisation of America. The situation of the bleekmen (the native Martians) is very similar to that of the original inhabitants of the American continent. On the planet, there is Camp Ben-Gurion, an institute for children with developmental disorders. At the institute, there is an autistic boy, Manfred Steiner. Manfred's father is convinced that his son's autism is due to his wife's lack of motherly talents, as she earned a master degree (sic) at the university. Manfred's psychiatrist is of a different opinion: to him, autism is innate and hence biological. This latter explanation is very modern and reminds us of the theories discussed earlier in the book. Dick describes it as follows:

> It assumes a derangement in the sense of time in the autistic individual, so that the environment around him is so accelerated that he cannot cope with it, in fact, he is unable to perceive it properly precisely as we would be if we faced a speeded-up television program, so that object whizzed by so fast as to be invisible, and sound was gobblegook.[13]

The main character, Jack Bohlen, had decided to emigrate to the vast plains of Mars because the urbanized environment of his home planet caused him to experience psychotic episodes. He has another relatively modern theory about autism:

> It was a battle, Jack realized, between the composite psyche of the school and the individual psyches of the children, and the former held all the key cards. A child who did not properly respond was assumed to be autistic, — that is, oriented according to a subjective factor that took precedence over his sense of objective reality. And that child wound up by being expelled from the school.[14]

Manfred Steiner is a non-verbal child who will only speak at the end of the novel when he is already living amongst the bleekmen. He indeed suffers from a distorted sense of time: the future and the present are

---

11   Kristien Hens and Raymond Langenberg, *Experiences of Adults Following an Autism Diagnosis* (Cham: Palgrave Macmillan, 2018).
12   Philip K. Dick, *Martian Time-Slip* (New York: Vintage Books, 1964).
13   Dick, *Martian Time-Slip*, p. 46.
14   Ibid., p. 75.

simultaneous for him. This paralyses him. His experience is of the simultaneousness of time, but also of not being able to come to terms with the progression of time. In another novel, written before his readers would have conceived of autism as a disorder of normal neurological development, the author describes a similar experience, albeit in a less science-fiction-like setting.

The first chapter of *The Sound and the Fury* (1929), by William Faulkner, narrates the experience of Benji Compson, a thirty-three-year-old man with an intellectual disability.[15] It is evident in the story that in his experience, present and past are intermixed. He does not distinguish between events that happened when he was a young child and events in the present, which eventually has tragic consequences. Both novels are refreshing because they describe the experiences of non-verbal people. They both depict an atypical sense of time, an experience that does not distinguish between present, past, and future. This atypical sense of time leads to the immediacy of experience, an immediacy that the rest of the environment does not share.

In my research into the experience of adults with a diagnosis of autism, people often talked about a different sense of time.[16] For example, one of the respondents said the following:

> What's typically me is that I'm never spontaneous and can't deal with unexpected issues. It's as if all stimuli first must pass through my brain and must be processed there. Everything has to be reasoned first. Because of this, my reactions can be delayed for a few seconds to a couple of minutes but are almost never spontaneous and uncontrolled. I also very often worry about the same thing for hours, months even.[17]

Experiences arrive slowly, but are then very intense. Another example is by Tatiana, who talks about a phone call she received when she was in Sardinia in a restaurant: her adult daughter had had a car accident. She survived, so Tatiana was told on the phone, and that reassured Tatiana. Only when she got home did she realise the seriousness of the situation, and she experienced very intense emotions. Only then did she call the hospital back. Another participant, Baukis, stated the following:

---

15   William Faulkner, *The Sound and the Fury* (New York: Knopf Doubleday Publishing Group, 1984).

16   Hens and Langenberg, *Experiences of Adults Following an Autism Diagnosis*.

17   Ibid., p. 30.

'For me, that is the essence of autism: that you need much more time and energy to connect all loose particles of information and come to the right conclusion.'[18] Another autistic person told me in a personal communication:

> I have a terrible short term memory but an excellent long term memory. Years can be mixed, and I remember casual conversations as if they happened yesterday.

What can we conclude from these testimonials? In the case of the people I interviewed, we can clearly see that the world is too fast for them, that their brains needs more time to process information, either because the information is absorbed at a very high intensity or because people get stuck on details. One of our respondents stated he would have preferred to go back to the seventeenth century, because everything was slower then. Instead of social media and its encouragement of immediate reactions, he wanted to go back to writing letters, where you take the time to respond. In the case of those fictional non-verbal characters mentioned above, they seem to make no distinction between present, past, and future. Perhaps all these experiences cannot be brought back to a single explanation. It seems that a sense of time is a function of the brain, and an atypically functioning brain can cause a conflict with a typical or 'normal' sense of time. In this respect, it is interesting that the people we interviewed also talked about disturbances in their circadian rhythm and challenges in estimating how long things will take. We may wonder whether it is an atypical sense of time that causes autistic behaviour and experiences or whether autism causes an atypical sense of time—although perhaps that question is nonsensical.

In ADHD, another developmental disorder, disturbances in one's sense of time have been discussed in more detail.[19] In thinking about ADHD, a specific term has been invented because people with this diagnosis often seem not to live according to the same timescale as people without ADHD: time blindness. People with ADHD, so it is

---

18   Ibid., p. 32.
19   John West, Graham Douglas, Stephen Houghton and Vivienne Lawrence, 'Time Perception in Boys with Attention-Deficit/Hyperactivity Disorder According to Time Duration, Distraction and Mode of Presentation', *Child Neuropsychology: A Journal on Normal and Abnormal Development in Childhood and Adolescence*, 6:4 (2000), 241–50, https://doi.org/10.1076/chin.6.4.241.3140

stated, live in the now and are driven by the now. Neurologists suggest that this may be related to some dysfunction of the frontal cortex: these people cannot organise their behaviour in relation to the future. Autistic people also sometimes describe the impossibility of imagining the future. Interestingly, this is not the only thing that autistic people and people with ADHD have in common. Both for ADHD and autism, people have explored visual thinking in the context of challenges in executive functioning and hypersensitivity. Perhaps this overlap in phenotype is an explanation for similar challenges related to a sense of time. We might wonder whether it is the more intense (or more visual) way people with ADHD and autistic people experience the world that causes a disturbance in their sense of time. It could be the case that neurodivergent people experience difficulties in sensing the flow of time that neurotypicals have implicitly agreed upon and are therefore less able to meet the requirements of a 'normal' sense of time. This book is not the right place to tackle these very fundamental questions. I will therefore end my speculation here and proceed to the ethical part of this chapter.

My earlier reflections might suggest that autistic people are confronted with significant difficulties because of their sense of time. If the world revolves too fast, how can one connect with a neurotypical person? Are autistic people permanently out of sync with neurotypical people? I do not think so. On the one hand, from my research, it is clear that autistic adults sometimes face significant challenges. However, these challenges do not have to lead to unintelligibility.[20] Many of us have experienced our brain reacting too slowly to input, or receiving too much input simultaneously, and becoming overloaded. Consider the following scenario: your friends have convinced you to have a drink after work; although you are exhausted, you agree and try to follow the discussion. However, you can only think about how tired you are and how you want to be alone. In such moments, your experience of time seems to progress more slowly than that of your friends. Think of the hundreds of work-related emails, Facebook messages, and texts you receive, so that you are always busy but do not manage to finish anything

---

20 See also: Thomas Fuchs and Hanne De Jaegher, 'Enactive Intersubjectivity: Participatory Sense-Making and Mutual Incorporation', *Phenomenology and the Cognitive Sciences*, 8:4 (2009), 465–86, https://doi.org/10.1007/s11097-009-9136-4

because your brain cannot process it all. I think this comes close to what autistic people experience regularly. Even when we concede that there is a cognitive basis to these challenges, it does not automatically mean that autistic people are fundamentally different or impossible to understand.

These observations should not lead to deterministic or reductionist thinking. Just because we might, in the future, know the biological or cognitive causes of an atypical sense of time, it does not mean that these challenges are insurmountable, a kind of lifelong punishment. It is indeed a risk rooted in assuming a biological cause of atypicality that it becomes a tragedy that you cannot avoid. There are no solutions besides learning to live with it.[21] Our respondents told me that they appreciated concrete solutions to concrete challenges. If there is a need during social interactions to have a faster reaction time in relation to other people, what could a practical solution be?

On the one hand, we need an appreciation that some people need more time than others and that others who do not experience these challenges should accommodate this and make more time. On the other hand, this might not be possible in all circumstances. In searching for the cause of such challenges, for example, searching for the gene for our circadian rhythm, we tend to forget that it is also relevant and necessary to find ways to transcend these challenges. For example, someone I talked to who had severe sleeping problems told me that her auticoach advised her to shower before going to bed and to put a pile of blankets on top of her, something she found very useful. There is a vast area of unknown terrain covering how executive functioning can be improved with tips and tricks, even if we consider the cause of the challenges as a genetic or brain atypicality. Even for those with conditions such as ADHD and dyslexia, who often find planning difficult, such training is hard to access or not made available. Moreover, trying to find ways in which neurodivergent people can tackle specific challenges they experience, and investigating and researching such approaches, is vastly different from 'curing autism'. I am vehemently opposed to suggestions that autism might or must be cured or trained away with invasive behavioural therapies. However, autistic people often point out that

---

21 Nomy Arpaly, 'How It Is Not "Just Like Diabetes": Mental Disorders and the Moral Psychologist', *Philosophical Issues*, 15:1 (2005), 282–98, https://doi.org/10.1111/j.1533-6077.2005.00067.x

embracing an autistic identity does not mean that one does not want help with certain aspects of functioning. Some of these challenges, such as sleeping problems, are difficult to tackle with support or acceptance alone. Respecting one other's vulnerability is a question of adapting one's own behaviour to accommodate another person, and recognizing a joint basis from which that person can be understood, to help them tackle challenges in such a way that they feel comfortable.

PART III: DYNAMICS OF AUTISM

Matter comes to matter – Karen Barad

9. Labels and Looping Effects

In chapter seven, we encountered Sandra, an autistic woman who experienced how her coworkers treated her differently after she received her diagnosis. She was given a different job that did not involve customer contact and was given a desk in a quiet office without coworkers, where she felt lonely. When we investigate the experiences of the parents of autistic children, we often notice similar dynamics. Child psychiatrist Delphine Jacobs performed an interview study with parents seeking a diagnostic assessment for their young children as part of her PhD. Although the parents thought that such a diagnosis would provide insight into their child's functioning, they also feared that teachers and other people's attitudes towards their child would change and that these people would consider their child as completely reduced to the label.[1] Professionals responsible for diagnoses also often talk about the uncertainties they experience regarding the impact of the label on children and adults.[2] Autistic adults, children, and parents of autistic children describe how a diagnostic label can provide insight and a better understanding of challenges. Nevertheless, Sandra's story and many parents' fears show that others can look at you differently

---

1 Delphine Jacobs, Jean Steyaert, Kris Dierickx, Kristien Hens, 'Parents' views and experiences of the Autism Spectrum Disorder diagnosis of their young child: a longitudinal interview study', *Child and Adolescent Psychiatry*, 29:8 (2019), 1143–54, http://www.doi.org/10.1007/s00787-019-01431-4; Delphine Jacobs, Jean Steyaert, Kris Dierickx, Kristien Hens, 'Parents' multi-layered expectations when requesting an Autism Spectrum Disorder assessment of their young child: an in-depth interview study', *BMC Psychiatry* 20:440 (2020), http://www.doi.org/10.1007/s00787-019-01431-4; https://doi.org/10.1186/s12888-020-02806-7

2 Delphine Jacobs, Jean Steyaert, Kris Dierickx, Kristien Hens, 'Physician View and Experience of the Diagnosis of Autism Spectrum Disorder in Young Children', *Frontiers in Psychiatry*, 10:372, (2019), https://doi.org/10.3389/fpsyt.2019.00372. Delphine Jacobs, Jean Steyaert, Kris Dierickx, Kristien Hens, 'Implications of an Autism Spectrum Disorder Diagnosis: An Interview Study of How Physicians Experience the Diagnosis in a Young Child', *J. Clin. Med.* 7:348 (2018).

  https://doi.org/10.11647/OBP.0261.09

when they know that you have a diagnosis. In this chapter, we shall discuss the impact of classifications on people and the impact of people on classifications. We will do so with the help of sociologist Erving Goffman and philosopher of science Ian Hacking.

Stigma and Looping:
The Thoughts of Erving Goffman and Ian Hacking

Many scholars have investigated the phenomenon of stigma that accompanies being labelled with a psychiatric diagnosis. The impact of a diagnosis, and hence of classification, has been elaborately described in labelling theory. Ian Hacking describes labelling theory as follows: '[it] asserts that social reality is conditioned, stabilized, or even created by the labels we apply to people, actions, and communities.'[3] One of the most well-known sociologists who has written about labelling theory is Erving Goffman. In his book *Stigma: Notes on the Management of Spoiled Identity*, he defines stigma as 'the situation of the individual who is disqualified from full social acceptance.'[4] The examples he gives are those of homosexuality, women in prostitution, drug addicts, or people who have been in a psychiatric institution or belong to a minority religion. Having a psychiatric label can also lead to stigma.

Such a stigma, according to Goffman, spoils someone's social identity: 'normals' do not take you seriously anymore. Even benevolent others or allies have difficulty seeing the person in question as more than their label, and one has to make an immense effort to encourage those people to do so again. The person who is labelled is considered different, expelled, and has to seek connection again. People who are benevolent towards outsiders may function as go-betweens between those stigmatised people and 'ordinary' people. People with a specific stigma also have similar learning experiences, a similar moral career. They start to see themselves in the same way as others see them and start to interpret past experiences in the same way. They start to behave like someone with a stigma. The fact that one is seen as different changes

---

3 Ian Hacking, *Historical Ontology* (Cambridge, Mass: Harvard University Press, 2004), p.103.

4 Erving Goffman, *Notes on the Management of Spoiled Identity* (New Jersey: Prentice Hall, 2009), p i.

one's self-insight, and the classification to which one belongs becomes an irrevocable part of one's identity. If you are labelled, you become your label.

A philosopher inspired by the work of Erving Goffman and Michel Foucault, and who has used autism extensively as an example, is Ian Hacking. Throughout his career, he has tried to position himself in his work relative to nominalism on the one hand and realism on the other. He describes this as follows:

> A traditional *nominalist* says that stars (or algae, or justice) have nothing in common with others of their kind except our names for them ("stars", "algae", "justice"). The traditional realist, in contrast, finds it amazing that the world could so kindly sort itself into our categories. He protests that there are definite sorts of objects in it, at least stars and algae, which we have painstakingly come to recognize and classify correctly.[5]

In an early paper, 'Making up People', that has been reworked and published as part of the book *Historical Ontology*, he suggests a dynamic nominalism:

> I believe that this sort of static nominalism is doubly wrong: I think that many categories come from nature, not from the human mind, and I think our categories are not static. A different kind of nominalism — I call it dynamic nominalism- attracts my realist self, spurred on by theories about the making of the homosexual and the heterosexual as kinds of persons or by my observations about official statistics. The claim of dynamic nominalism is not that there was a kind of person who was increasingly to be recognized by bureaucrats or by students of human nature, but rather that a kind of person came into being at the same time as the kind itself was invented.[6]

Hacking tells us that kinds of people started to exist at specific points in history and that they could disappear later on. The hysteric, as she was considered in the nineteenth century, is probably an excellent example of this. Considering what we have investigated in chapter four about the origins of autism in the middle of the previous century, it is not difficult to see why the concept of autism has drawn Hacking's attention.

---

5   Hacking, *Historical Ontology*, p. 104.
6   Ibid., p. 106.

How does this dynamic nominalism work? In his chapter 'The Looping Effects of Human Kinds',[7] Hacking elaborates on this further. By 'human kinds', a term he will abandon later on, he means kinds of people (not individual people): their behaviour, types of emotions, experiences, etc. These kinds are defined and studied in the human sciences. We would like to have exact information about these kinds, but we do not have it. Human kinds are, therefore, different from genes or quarks. These we could call, with American philosopher Willard Quine (1908–2000), natural kinds. However, we might prefer it if human kinds corresponded to natural kinds—for example, it might make some discussions easier if we could map the human kind called 'woman' one-on-one with a natural (and biological) kind. However, we have known for a long time that this is not possible. Autism is a human kind: psychologists and psychiatrists study it. It seems that scientific researchers of autism are eager to make sure that it will become a natural kind, but human kinds are not mere natural kinds of which we do not know the cause yet. They are also not necessarily social constructs that we mix up with kinds. As with natural kinds, we try to look for the causes of human kinds, and we try to explain them.

Still, human kinds are different from natural kinds. They are not value-free. People do not wish to be human kinds because they have moral import. Hacking gives the example of 'child abuser' as an example of such a human kind to which we do not want to belong. Nevertheless, by offering biological explanations for them, human kinds are often reduced to natural kinds, and people belonging to a certain kind are 'exculpated'. Think, for example, about genetic explanations for addiction. Hacking's most notable contribution to understanding human kinds is probably his remark that human kinds are subject to what Hacking calls looping effects. Being classified changes people in the future, but the past of the classified person also becomes reinterpreted. 'Being classified' changes how people think about themselves and how they will act. Because classified people change, this will eventually mean that the classification itself will also change. If what we know about a classification changes, this will, in turn, have consequences for people belonging to the classification: the looping will go on and on.

---

7   Ian Hacking, 'The Looping Effects of Human Kinds', in *Causal Cognition*, ed. by Dan Sperber, David Premack, and Ann James Premack (Oxford: Oxford University Press, 1996), pp. 351–83.

In *The Social Construction of What?* Hacking describes social constructionism: in chapter four ('Madness: Biological or Constructed?'); he discusses autism to illustrate the effect of classifications. [8] He states that we cannot quickly answer what has an essence and what is construed by language. He uses the words of Hillary Putnam to express that

> [...] a *common* philosophical error of supposing that 'reality' must refer to a single super thing, instead of looking at the ways we endlessly renegotiate- and are *forced* to renegotiate — our notion of reality as our language and our life develops.[9]

Hacking himself looks for a more nuanced approach to what exists solely in language and what is real. Instead of using human kinds, he uses the term interactive kinds in this chapter, in contrast to things like quarks, which he calls indifferent kinds. The term interactive applies to the people categorised and the classifications, the kinds to which they belong. They interact with what they classify. This can imply that people who belong to a particular classification will start to behave according to the classification's descriptions. However, we must be aware that classification also occurs in a larger context of institutions and practices. Children with ADHD are, for example, put in a room without much distraction. The classification 'hyperactive' not only influences these children because they are aware that they are considered to be so, but also because they are put in an environment for hyperactive children. If these children were not aware of their diagnosis, this diagnosis would still influence their environment and thus their behaviour.

Hacking is very interested in the example of autism, precisely because you could consider it as an interactive and an indifferent kind at the same time. I have already described autism as a striking example of the tension between 'real' and 'a social construct'. For Hacking, autism is undoubtedly also a biological-neurological condition. He states that autistic children are, at first glance, perhaps a problematic example of an interactive kind. Autistic children often have communication challenges, and some may not be aware that they are classified as autistic. Nevertheless, just as with the example of ADHD, the fact that they are put in a specific setting deemed appropriate for autistic children

---

8   Ian Hacking, *The Social Construction of What?* (Cambridge, Mass: Harvard University Press, 2001).

9   Hacking, *The Social Construction of What?*, p. 101.

influences them. They often receive special education, and when they attend regular classes, from the moment they are diagnosed they are often assigned someone who helps them and suggests appropriate support. The matrix of practices in which the child is put, regardless of whether she is aware of her diagnosis, changes irrevocably, and this will affect the child herself.

Hacking later describes a thought experiment. What if we, at a specific moment, discover pathology P, the biological essence of autism. This could be a gene or something in the brain:

> How would the discovery of P affect how autistic children and their families conceive of themselves; how would it affect their behaviour? What would be the looping affect [sic] on the stereotype of autistic children? Which children, formerly classified as autistic, would now be excluded, and what would that do to them?[10]

There is indeed something inherently dangerous in wanting to fix autism within a yet-to-be-discovered biological reality. Some children and adults who were previously considered autistic or who considered themselves to be autistic would probably be excluded from this diagnosis. We can only wonder what that would do to people who have come to see autism as an appropriate way to think about their own functioning. If we were to discover pathology P and pin this down as the essence of autism, we would fundamentally change what autism *is* now: a diagnosis based on behavioural characteristics, flexible, and hence workable.

In a later article, 'Kinds of People: Moving Targets,' Ian Hacking refers again to the example of autism.[11] In this article, Hacking wants to provide a framework about how we should think about the fact that classifications create new kinds of people and about the fact that classifications and those classified are susceptible to the looping effect. He abandons the idea of natural versus human kinds and talks instead about kinds of people. We often assume that kinds of people are predefined categories with fixed characteristics. If we get to know these characteristics better, we can control and adjust them. However, that is not how it works, according to Hacking. Kinds of people are moving targets: we interact with them as we study them, and therefore they change. They are no

---

10   Ibid., p. 121.
11   Ian Hacking, 'Kinds of People: Moving Targets', in *Proceedings of the British Academy*, Volume 151, 2006 Lectures (2007), pp. 285–318.

longer the same kinds of people as before. This is the looping effect: the science we undertake also creates kinds of people. Human sciences such as psychology and psychiatry study kinds of people. We want to measure and know and hopefully find biological causes. Nevertheless, it is not only by giving kinds of people a classification that dynamics of looping come to exist. The people classified, the experts who do the classification, and the institutions and knowledge about classifications: all of these interact with and contribute to creating kinds of people. Therefore, Hacking's nominalism is dynamic.

A classification also enables people to think about themselves in a specific historical context. Hacking refers to Foucault's example of homosexuality. There have always been homosexual acts, but only recently have people started to think about themselves as homosexual, and only recently has homosexuality become a sexual orientation and a way of being. The applicability of this way of thinking to autism is clear. It is only since Kanner and Asperger have started describing certain children as autistic that people have started to see them as autistic, and adults and children have been able to see themselves as autistic.

Furthermore, although there have always been people with what we now see as autistic traits, autism has only recently become a way of being. Moreover, the stories that autistic people tell about their own experiences change how autism is defined. Think about the specific sensory sensibilities of autistic people. For a long time they have not been considered as core symptoms. Since the DSM-5, however, they are included as a diagnostic criterion, probably because of the influence of autistic people themselves. The classification itself has changed by adding a new criterion: the collection of people classified now may not precisely overlap with the collection of people classified in the past.

In his writing, Hacking gives an original description of the relationship between language and reality, between classification and those classified. However, I believe he cannot wholly solve the dialectic between social construct and reality. He talks about biolooping, in which certain interactive and indifferent types interact with one another. Specific ideas about autism, the idea that it is a condition that we should treat with behavioural therapy, for example, will influence people's brains through this behavioural therapy. Other ideas will have a different influence on the brain. But what happens when classifications change the classified?

Is the distinction between biolooping and classificatory looping useful? Could classificatory looping also change something in the biology of the person classified? Hacking leaves these questions open.

Looping Genomes

Hacking's dynamic nominalism is an exciting way to reflect on autism. In a fascinating article by Daniel Navon and Gil Eyal, 'Looping Genomes: Diagnostic Change and the Genetic Makeup of the Autism Population',[12] both authors describe how knowledge about the genetic origins of a diagnostic category interacts with the kinds of people that people believe fall under the diagnostic category. They demonstrate how the search for a genetic explanation of autism has contributed to the diagnostic expansion of autism. They do this by looking at the number of autism diagnoses in research cohorts that are selected based on genetic mutations. In this way, they seek to demonstrate that, at present, because the diagnostic criteria have changed, genetic mutations that previously did not fall under the diagnosis of autism now do so. It is a dynamic process: genetic findings have caused a shift in diagnostic criteria. People who clinicians and researchers previously considered to have a specific genetic mutation are now considered autistic. For example, people who were previously considered to have Phelan McDermid syndrome increasingly receive a diagnosis of autism. The authors describe four loops that have contributed to the fact that autism has transformed from a rare disorder to a frequent, heritable, and genetic heterogeneous spectrum of communicative and social disorders. They point at the importance of genetisation for the entire process of considering autism more and more as a genetic condition.

The first loop starts with Leo Kanner, who saw similarities between parents and their children. This has led to the fact that scholars primarily see autism as something genetic, especially thanks to Bernard Rimland (the second loop), who opposed psychogenic explanations of autism, and who found in genes the explanation for these intra-familial similarities. Nevertheless, autism being considered a genetic condition

---

12   Daniel Navon and Gil Eyal, 'Looping Genomes: Diagnostic Change and the Genetic Makeup of the Autism Population', *AJS; American Journal of Sociology*, 121 (2016), 1416–71.

is also an attractive diagnosis for parents. If something is genetic, parents are not directly responsible for their children's challenges. It has a destigmatising effect. Twin studies in the seventies formed the third loop, which indeed showed that autism was heritable. Through this, the Broader Autism Phenotype was discovered: people who had autistic traits but did not fulfil all diagnostic criteria. These were often family members of people with a diagnosis. Diagnostic criteria were widened to make autism into a broad spectrum. However, because more people fit the diagnostic criteria, autism became more heterogeneous with respect to the underlying genetics: the number of mutations detected in cohorts of people with a diagnosis rose.

From the 1990s onwards, fundamental research into autism genes took off. This was partly due to parents' organisations, to whom it was essential that researchers discovered genetic causes of autism. They subsequently found more genetic mutations because these were actively sought after and because the population of diagnosed people became more heterogeneous. Navon and Eyal give the example of Fragile-X. This is a genetic condition that is today associated with autism. However, this has not always been the case: in the early days of research, a diagnosis of autism and Fragile-X were mutually exclusive. Only in DSM-III did it become possible to diagnose intellectual impairment and autism together. Because people could now think of these two as being linked, and because clinicians no longer considered autistic aloneness as a base characteristic of autism but rather spoke in terms of social and communicative problems, autism as a diagnosis could also apply to persons with Fragile-X syndrome. And indeed, children with Fragile-X do sometimes exhibit repetitive behaviour and experience challenges with language development. However, they also have strong social awareness, which we might not have expected in the original children Kanner observed. By linking Fragile-X and autism, the genetic research into both phenomena was connected: researchers could work together on theories about the pathways from genetics to behaviour. The autism community could hope that there would eventually be a biological explanation for autistic behaviour.

Moreover, parents of children with Fragile-X gained access to therapies that were aimed at autistic people. Simultaneously, Fragile-X researchers gained access to research funding that was intended for research into autism genes. Fragile-X became a biological model for autism. Other examples are Phelan-McDermid syndrome, which is caused by a deletion in chromosome 22. These people have mild to severe cognitive disability and language impairment. Until recently, the syndrome was not associated with autism. Furthermore, because these people were often cognitively challenged, it was argued that — although they might have some autistic traits — it was not meaningful to talk about 'real' autism in these cases. In 2008, autism was seen as an adequate diagnosis for people with this syndrome, long after the diagnostic criteria for autism were extended in DSM-IV. This shift is probably due to the example of Fragile-X. If a genetic syndrome is associated with autism, it gives syndrome researchers access to a broad community of autism researchers, with efficient access to research funding for autism research. Moreover, people with family members with Phelan-McDermid were motivated to contribute to autism research. There was something in it for both sides.

One of the most striking examples is Williams syndrome. Until 2000, this syndrome was positioned as the opposite of autism. People with Williams syndrome are hypersocial and have strong communicative skills. However, today, more and more people with Williams syndrome are diagnosed with autism. Diagnosticians interpret their social skills as only superficial: being too social can be seen as a social deficit as well. Besides these examples that Navon and Eyal have described, I think we will see these mechanisms increasingly at work with ADHD and autism. ADHD and autism sometimes occur together, but ADHD is more readily seen as a behavioural problem. Often people with ADHD are very social and communicative. Anecdotal evidence suggests that some psychiatrists look for a more in-depth explanation for ADHD, and, in some cases, they consider ADHD to be an expression of underlying autism. If you have ADHD, you can also be 'too social'. Autism as a diagnosis may be preferable for some parents: to the outside world, ADHD is still often seen essentially as annoying behaviour; autism is a way of being that is perceived to have good and bad sides. Time will tell if my prediction is correct.

At the beginning of this book, I described how autism, which we conceive of as a neurobiological phenomenon, has acquired different meanings throughout its history. I also suggested that autism is more than a condition. For many people, it is part of their identity. In this chapter, I have discussed several authors who have investigated these mechanisms. Erving Goffman described the phenomenon of stigma: how a label becomes part of how you and others understand yourself. Ian Hacking has investigated how classifications alter those classified, and how those classified alter the classifications themselves. Gil Eyal and Dan Navon have applied this idea to the association between genetic syndromes and autism. Although the relationship between genes and autism seems straightforward — genes 'explain' autism — their paper demonstrates that other mechanisms contribute to classifications and objects of study. Erving Goffman was a sociologist; Ian Hacking is a philosopher of science. If the classification has such a profound effect on people, what kind of ethical implications does this have? We might ask ourselves if we should make these decisions for other people, specifically for young children. How do we weigh the advantages of a diagnosis with the disadvantages of stigma? Perhaps diagnosticians have a duty to communities as a whole and to actively strive to educate the greater public to remove the stigma, so that the association between specific diagnoses and stigma is no longer there. However, even without stigma, having a specific label also changes the ways other people look at and treat those who are classified. It is a life-course-changing event. I will later come back to the question of how we should deal with this. In the next chapter, we will further investigate dynamic conceptions of the relationship between people, between organism and environment, and between language and reality.

10. Dynamic Approaches

In the first part of this book, we discussed the different levels of meaning of autism. Autism is a psychiatric diagnosis that is given based on criteria in diagnostic manuals such as the DSM. Autism can be considered a disability and identity. Autism is a phenomenon that is also historical: the diagnosis has come into being in a specific place and time. Simultaneously, autism is also a set of characteristics that some people probably always had, fixed in their biology. Crip Theory offered a vision of disability that made space for polysemous and often shifting meanings. According to this vision, we can think of disability as something corporeal and something that is socially constructed. Labelling theory and Ian Hacking's dynamic nominalism demonstrate how diagnoses can change a specific diagnosed individual and the group of diagnosed people, and how they can change the diagnosis. This chapter will describe how, in other fields, such as biology, we can use more dynamic concepts. I will use the ideas of doctor and philosopher Georges Canguilhem (1904–1995), who called for a more dynamic conception of pathology as early as the middle of the last century. Then I will explain enactivist approaches of the human mind and their application to autism, before concluding with a short description of new materialism and the ideas of Karen Barad.

Dynamics of Health and Disease: Georges Canguilhem

It is perhaps not a particularly radical idea that autism should not solely be seen as a problem within the individual, but also always in relation to others. We have, however, already discussed that autism is also seen as one of the more biological psychiatric diagnoses. This confers certain

 https://doi.org/10.11647/OBP.0261.10

advantages: the more biologically anchored something is thought to be, the more real it is deemed to be: the person with a diagnosis of autism receives the recognition that the challenges he or she experiences are real, that they are not imaginary, and that they are unavoidable. The biological conception is deculpabilising. People will tolerate particular behaviour more readily from someone diagnosed with autism than from someone without such a diagnosis. A diagnosis that we think about as biological also has the advantage that one is more forgiving about one's own failures. A disadvantage of such a physical conception of psychiatric diagnosis is that it often leads to reductionism: the person is reduced to their genes. There is not much room for development or their own agency. However, it is possible that the association between biologically fixed and psychological malleable, which is often assumed in many conceptions about autism, is not warranted. I will describe some thinkers who have developed dynamic conceptions of biology and the human mind in what follows.

Georges Canguilhem may be one of the most original thinkers about life and health as dynamic and interactive. He was a medical doctor and philosopher and has gained some fame as Michel Foucault's tutor. Nevertheless, he deserves some attention himself, as he has a refreshing and modern view of pathologies. Canguilhem has a biological conception of pathology, but argues that illness and pathology have to do with the individual's experiences of suffering related to their relationship with their environment. With Canguilhem, we return to a discussion introduced in chapter two: what is a disease, and when is something a disease, and to what extent can our intuitions say something about this? We have seen that Christopher Boorse tried to pin this down objectively by referring to the concept of species-typical functioning.[1] Jerome Wakefield thought that psychiatric conditions resulted from an evolutionary function that has gone awry and is now considered disordered.[2] We asked ourselves to what extent we can offer a naturalistic explanation of the difference between suffering and health. Perhaps calling something a disease is, in the first place, something normative.

---

1   Christopher Boorse, 'Health as a Theoretical Concept', *Philosophy of Science*, 44:4 (1977), 542–73.

2   Jerome C. Wakefield, 'The Concept of Mental Disorder: Diagnostic Implications of the Harmful Dysfunction Analysis', *World Psychiatry*, 6:3 (2007), 149–56.

Canguilhem approaches this question using empirical data about how organisms function.[3] His most famous work is *The Normal and the Pathological* (1943). He argues that the pathological is not merely a quantitative deviation from the normal situation but a qualitative one: all functions work differently in a pathological condition.[4] He concedes that looking at the pathological as a broken version of the normal has certain advantages: it suggests that we must try to repair the statistically normal by targeted interventions with medication. However, this is not correct. If we want to know what is pathological, we have to look for what is going on in the state of the disease. We cannot merely extrapolate this state from the normal condition:

> There is no objective pathology. Structures or behaviours can be objectively described but they cannot be called "pathological" on the strength of some purely objective criterion. Objectively, only varieties or differences can be defined with positive or negative vital values.[5]

Canguilhem gives the example of diabetes: this is not merely the presence of statistically higher glucose, but the cooperation of different factors: the circulatory system, the nervous system, the endocrine system; they all work differently as a reaction to changes in movement or food. We have to look at the pathological as a different kind of 'normal', a condition that can stand on its own and where other norms prevail. As a result, the normal state can no longer function as the reference point to see whether something is normal or pathological:

> if the normal does not have the rigidity of a fact of collective constraint, but rather the flexibility of a norm which is transformed in its relation to individual conditions, it is clear that the boundary between the normal and the pathological becomes imprecise.[6]

We may wonder, then, what makes something pathological if we cannot deduce it by measurements alone? Here, Canguilhem introduces the concept of biological normativity, a normativity in relation to the adaptation to the environment: it is their relationship that makes them

---

3   Jonathan Sholl, 'Escaping the Conceptual Analysis Straitjacket: Pathological Mechanisms and Canguilhem's Biological Philosophy', *Perspectives in Biology and Medicine*, 58:4 (2015), 395–418, https://doi.org/10.1353/pbm.2015.0032

4   Georges Canguilhem, *The Normal and the Pathological* (New York: Zone Books, 1989).

5   Canguilhem, *The Normal and the Pathological*, p. 226.

6   Ibid., p. 182.

such. Organisms adapt to their environment or try to adapt to their environment to survive in it. Health means being able to dynamically adjust to the current situation, but also to changing situations. Health is therefore the margin of tolerance to change:

> Being healthy means being not only normal in a given situation, but also normative in this and other eventual [sic] situations. What characterizes health is the possibility of transcending the norm, which defines the momentary normal, the possibility of tolerating infractions of the habitual normal and instituting new norms in new situations. (...) Health is a margin of tolerance for the inconstancies of the environment.[7]

The norms Canguilhem talks about are biological. They are the adaptations that the individual makes to itself or to its milieu in order to survive. They are, therefore, temporary norms. They can be propulsive if the organism can define new norms and adapt to new circumstances, or repulsive if the organism has to do everything in its power to maintain the current situation. Because of this combination of propulsivity and repulsivity, we consider things to be normal or pathological. An organism is in a dynamic interaction with its environment, and within this interaction, new situations occur that we consider 'ill' or 'healthy'. We consider disease to be a negative biological experience: we perceive ourselves as healthy if our organism is resilient to change in the environment (propulsive). We perceive ourselves as ill if our organism is less resilient to changes (repulsive). Pathology and health are hence systemic properties. It is an individual assessment of the current situation in which one suffers. This does not mean that the pathology is actually 'in' the individual. Pathology arises when there is a mismatch between the individual and their environment, and if the individual cannot repair this mismatch by itself. For example, someone with low blood pressure at sea level is healthy when they are in the mountains because they will experience no suffering. Science may explain a specific experience of illness by pointing out where the mismatch lies. But medicine, as it deals with disease and health, operates at the level of experience, not merely at the level of causation.[8]

---

7   Ibid.
8   Anna M. T. Bosman, 'Disorders Are Reduced Normativity Emerging from the Relationship Between Organisms and Their Environment', in *Parental Responsibility in the Context of Neuroscience and Genetics*, International Library of Ethics,

In her paper 'Disorders Are Reduced Normativity Emerging from the Relationship Between Organisms and Their Environment,' Anna Bosman applies Canguilhem's ideas to psychiatric illness.[9] She starts her paper by explaining what a correct measurement is, referring here to an article about validity by Denny Borsboom and colleagues.[10] Measuring temperature is, for example, proper if the measurement denotes a change in kinetic energy in the environment. But what does this mean for psychological tests such as IQ tests or ADOS-2 that try to measure autistic traits? Firstly, we have to know what is measured. We have already discussed at length that this is not entirely clear in the case of autism. It is not hard to understand that it is probably also difficult in the case of intelligence. Firstly, then, we need a theory of what autism is.

Nevertheless, even if we take a simple view about, for example, autism or intelligence, Bosman states that we still have a problem. How can we decide whether something is too high or too low? How can we decide in psychiatry when phenomena deviate from the standard to such a degree that they become disorders? If we talk about temperature, this always happens in a specific situation: fifty degrees Celsius is too hot for your bath but too cold to cook potatoes. In IQ tests, the norms are already built in: below a certain point (seventy), it is assumed that you cannot easily take part in general education. With a high ADOS score, we believe that the person in question will experience some difficulties in social situations. The person is then considered 'not normal' in that respect.

Statistics cannot help us to decide at which point someone is objectively too intelligent or insufficiently intelligent. It is crucial here to return to Canguilhem's idea: a healthy organism is an organism that can adapt itself dynamically and with a certain freedom to the environment, and that can adjust the milieu to its norms. Pathology means not being able to adapt and not being able to tolerate change. It is perhaps tempting to link this to the idea that autistic people cannot tolerate change and are intrinsically pathological. However, such

Law, and the New Medicine (Cham: Springer, 2017), pp. 35–54, https://doi.org/10.1007/978-3-319-42834-5_3

9   Bosman, 'Disorders Are Reduced Normativity', pp. 35–54.

10   Denny Borsboom, Gideon J. Mellenbergh, and Jaap van Heerden, 'The Concept of Validity', *Psychological Review*, 111:4 (2004), 1061–71, https://doi.org/10.1037/0033-295X.111.4.1061

an argument goes against the views of Canguilhem, who explicitly considered pathology and health in relation to the environment. Hence, an autistic person who does not tolerate change very well is perfectly healthy in a predictable environment. Someone with ADHD is perfectly healthy in an environment in which they do not have to sit still. Healthy organisms are also organisms that can create new norms and adapt their environment to their own needs. Someone susceptible to sensory stimuli is healthy in an environment where they can shut down these stimuli. Children having difficulties sitting still are perfectly healthy if they can control when they can sit still and when they need to stand up or move. Being introverted is only pathological in a classroom where a teacher expects you to talk every morning. Therefore, medical professionals must listen to a patient's experiences of suffering in his or her environment rather than simply examining the physical condition of the individual. A doctor, according to Canguilhem, should first and foremost take care of the suffering person.

Enactivist Approaches to Autism

Anna Bosman describes Canguilhem as a precursor of complex adaptive systems thinking. Complex adaptive systems are systems such as organisms, immune systems, brains, and insect colonies: they can learn and adapt and are emergent: we cannot reduce them to their parts. In *Mind in Life. Biology, Phenomenology, and the Sciences of Mind*, Evan Thompson describes an 'enactive' approach to the mind.[11] In such a system, the human mind emerges from processes that organise themselves and connect the brain, body, and environment on different levels. A human being is just like other living creatures, and their parts are a self-determining system that creates a dynamic relationship to the environment, creating and maintaining its own identity. In such 'autopoiesis' the embodied self appears, and together with it the world with which it interacts. This process of autopoiesis is a process of sense-making, giving meaning to oneself and the world. Furthermore, this sense-making is 'enaction': it is oriented to and subject to the environment. This approach explicitly opposes the idea

---

11   Evan Thompson, *Mind in Life: Biology, Phenomenology, and the Sciences of Mind* (Cambridge, Mass: Harvard University Press, 2007).

of human beings as atomistic and isolated, against the idea of brains as computers and genes as blueprints. Our consciousness is embodied and exists in relation to the environment. This creates and is created in a dynamic process. Suppose we assume that life and consciousness are indeed dynamic processes that generate meaning and receive meaning. In that case, we can also understand the importance of phenomenology, studying experiences and sense-making, if we want to study the human mind.[12]

Hanne De Jaegher has applied this line of thinking to autism in her paper 'Embodiment and Sense-Making in Autism'.[13] According to this approach, embodiment, experience, and social interaction are the key to understanding autism. The approach is also comprehensive; she tries to bring together senso-motoric, cognitive, sensory, and affective aspects of autism in a framework. This approach aims to build bridges between autistic people and their environment and ameliorate their quality of life. She refers to research that does not consider autism solely as a social and communicative challenge. She also defines autism as a different way of perceiving and moving. In this way, she wants to put the experience of autistic people at the centre of her work, and to investigate how autistic people create sense in the world.

She talks about participatory sense-making: individual sense-making is influenced by coordination with other individuals. By aligning our movements, emotions, and interactions with others, and by being thus coupled, we are part of each other's sense-making. We are in sync. Think about musicians who automatically synchronize and coordinate their play. The interaction itself makes sense-making possible. We can then see autism as a difference in embodiment. Autistic people sometimes react more slowly or less visibly when viewing a movement. It feels to them that the world goes too fast. Some have suggested that autistic people have heightened perception. Because there are motor and sensory differences in autistic people, this will influence their participatory sense-making. If autistic people react more slowly to certain behaviours than their non-autistic respondents, it will be more challenging to become in

---

12   For a good overview of enactivist approaches to autism, see: Janna Van Grunsven, 'Perceiving "Other" Minds: Autism, 4E Cognition, and the Idea of Neurodiversity', *The Journal of Consciousness Studies*, 27:7-8 (2020), 115–43.

13   Hanne De Jaegher, 'Embodiment and Sense-Making in Autism', *Frontiers in Integrative Neuroscience*, 7 (2013), https://doi.org/10.3389/fnint.2013.00015, 1–19.

sync. However, they can acquire a rhythm of participatory sense-making with other autistic people. This allows us to understand that certain autistic behaviours, for example, repetitive behaviours such as flapping hands, which in the context of autism are often called stimming, are part of the way autistic people generate meaning. Echolalia, repeating another person's expressions, can be a way to maintain oneself as an autonomous individual in a conversation.

This approach to autism also has ethical consequences. Rather than considering specific behaviour to be disturbing or abnormal, we have to assume that it has a meaning for the person in question and that we have to try to grasp this meaning. The use of music can, for example, enable autistic children and their non-autistic respondents to find the right rhythm in social interaction and communication. In any case, De Jaegher ends by saying: 'Ethically, the point forward is not one of *laissez-faire*. On the contrary, it is one that starts from *also* taking the perspective and subjectivity of autistic people themselves seriously, in a principled, coherent, and comprehensive way. It is then that we can expect to be able to build bridges that are well-informed by both autistic and non-autistic experience.'[14]

Karen Barad and New Materialism

Dynamic and enactivist models of life and mind offer us the opportunity to look differently at autism. If we take them seriously, we are no longer talking about autistic people as individuals with fundamental shortcomings in their genes or the software or hardware of their brain. On the one hand, this allows us to conceive of autism as a phenomenon that appears in interaction with a given context, as a meaningful reaction to specific environments. On the other hand, it also provides us with a guideline for sensible research. The experiences of autistic people become equally important to those approaches as those of non-autistic people. However, looking dynamically at a phenomenon that we have long considered static also has ethical consequences. I shall come back to this later.

One thinker who views ontology, epistemology, and ethics as inextricably intertwined is Karen Barad. She is a professor in feminist

---

14　De Jaegher, 'Embodiment and Sense-Making in Autism', p. 19.

studies, philosophy, and history of consciousness at the University of California in Santa Cruz and one of the most well-known theoreticians of new materialism. New materialism is a line of thought in a philosophy that tries to transcend the dichotomy between language and reality. This dichotomy is not solved by more traditional materialist approaches nor by poststructuralist methods. The approach is interdisciplinary and has affinities with gender studies, disability studies, and environmental studies, and it reconceptualises nature and matter as dynamic and agentic.[15] Barad is a physicist by training and has a PhD in quantum physics. In her book *Meeting the Universe Halfway* (2007), she describes one of the starting points of new materialism.[16] New materialists do not continue to wrestle with nominalism and essentialism, with social constructionism and biological realness. Instead, they state that everything is matter: matter is what matters. There is no difference between representation and underlying matter. However, contrary to more traditional forms of materialism, this vision does not lead to naive reductionism or determinism.

Barad developed her ideas based on her reading of Niels Bohr's interpretation of quantum theory and states that 'quantum theory leads us out of the morass that takes absolutism and relativism to be the only two possibilities'.[17] The uncertainty principle states that particles may have a locality and momentum, but we cannot know them. Barad says that for Bohr, it is more than that; it is uncertainty *and* indeterminacy. Particles do not have momentum and location simultaneously, and the fact that we cannot perceive these characteristics simultaneously is not only the result of our observation. The act of knowing itself will determine one of the features (location/momentum). There is, besides an epistemic uncertainty, also an ontological indeterminacy. There is no original object with inaccessible characteristics, only phenomena. Furthermore, these phenomena are continuously produced at the quantum level and the macro level. It is, according to Barad, absurd to think that the quantum world is ruled by other physical laws than our

---

15 Stacy Alaimo, Susan Hekman, and Susan J. Hekman, *Material Feminisms* (Bloomington: Indiana University Press, 2008).

16 Karen Barad, *Meeting the Universe Halfway: Quantum Physics and the Entanglement of Matter and Meaning* (Durham & London: Duke University Press, 2007).

17 Barad, *Meeting the Universe Halfway*, p. 18.

visible world. She suggests because these ideas come from quantum physics does not mean that they do not apply to our world.

With our practices in our daily lives, we can make things real, and we produce bodies and meanings: matter comes to matter. Differences and categories come into existence by the daily practice in which we use them. By labelling someone autistic, we also create the autistic person, and this has always been the case. However, contrary to Bohr and later quantum physicists, who have sometimes assigned a special status to the human mind, Barad is no strict humanist. In this process of creating differences and meanings, the human being has no special status. Barad considers herself to be a posthumanist, not in the sense of transhumanist, but in the sense that people are not exceptional. Human beings are also emerging phenomena of the world, a world that is continuously becoming. We are part of the nature we try to understand. She uses the term agential realism. This is realism, not in the sense that words and things map one-on-one, but as an explanation of how discursive practices are linked to material phenomena. She states that 'practices of knowing are specific material entanglements that participate in reconfiguring the world.'[18] For her, theoretical concepts are specific physical arrangements. If we refer back to Hacking's description of looping effects, we can understand this: by mattering (which gives meaning to something), we create boundaries and realise phenomena. Barad transcends Hacking's distinction between human kind and natural kind: all phenomena are materialist and dynamic, always becoming through intra-action with one another. Barad uses the term intra-action rather than interaction. With this term, she tries to explain that pairs such as subject/object, thing/word, ontology/epistemology are not independent because they act upon each other from the beginning. They bring each other into being in and through the intra-actions between and inside of the action.

We bring into being the autistic child or the autistic adult through diagnosis, and through this, the other path (the future without a diagnosis) is closed off. It is not merely a name or a description that we give to someone. For Barad, it is also intrinsically an ethical act: we make realities and close down other possibilities by our practices. We have to account for that. This is ethics situated in praxis. In this regard,

---

18   Ibid., p. 91.

in their edited volume, *Material Feminisms*, Stacy Alaimo and Susan Hekman say:

> A material ethics entails, on the contrary, that we can compare the very real material consequences of ethical positions and draw conclusions from those comparisons. We can, for example, argue that the material consequences of one ethics is more conclusive to human and nonhuman *flourishing* than that of another. *Furthermore*, material ethics allows us to shift the focus from ethical principles to ethical practices. Practices are, by nature, *embodied, situated actions*.[19]

Barad and others leave the discussion of nominalism/ representationalism/essentialism behind, favouring a dynamic and not deterministic materialism, which is at the same time normative. This approach seems a valuable way to look at diagnoses as well. It allows us to look at autism simultaneously as a historical and lived experience and as something real. Thus, we can leave behind ethics that one-sidedly uses generally applicable principles, instead favouring ethics embedded in concrete clinical and scientific practice.

In the previous chapter, we explored dynamic approaches on different levels. With the help of George Canguilhem, we described a dynamic and context-sensitive approach to pathology. Something becomes pathological in relation to an environment in which it cannot maintain itself. This leads to the experience of suffering. With the help of Hanne De Jaegher, we explored an enactive approach to the mind in general, and autism in particular: sense-making happens in coordination with others and should not be considered individualistically. With Karen Barad, matter itself becomes dynamic, and the distinction of language versus essence or word versus thing stops making sense. Our words, our praxis matter, even literally. This has profound ethical consequences. With our words and praxis, we enable or disable possible futures. Hence, they require careful consideration. In the next chapter, I will return to what has historically been conceived of as the matter, the static and unmoveable essence of autism: the gene. I will explore how we can also think of genes as dynamic.

---

19   Stacy Alaimo, Susan Hekman, *Material Feminisms* (Bloomington: Indiana University Press, 2008), p. 7.

11. Autism and Genetics

This book has described different layers of the meaning of autism, ranging from psychiatric diagnosis to neurodevelopmental disorder to neurological identity. We have seen how, even from its inception, the two founding fathers of autism, Leo Kanner and Hans Asperger, conceive of autism's essence differently. Although the children they described probably had the same phenotypical characteristics, autism was a child psychiatric and developmental phenomenon for Kanner. He described how behaviour gradually changed over time, how the children 'extended 'their cautious feelers'.[1] For Asperger, autism was firmly rooted in one's personality: he saw it as a trait, or even a disorder, with which one is born and dies. Autism, as a psychiatric diagnosis based on behavioural observation and an assessment of someone's functioning, allows for certain flexibility: strictly speaking, not everyone with specific cognitive or emotional characteristics needs to receive a diagnosis of autism if these characteristics do not lead to suffering or dysfunction. Nevertheless, in everyday language and scientific papers, autism is often called an innate, genetic, and lifelong developmental disorder.

When considering autism, we often think about specific characteristics or peculiarities that a person might have, which might pose some challenges for them. Moreover, autistic adults often testify about how autism is intrinsically linked with their identity. Since the beginning of the history of autism as we know it, people have considered it a biological disorder. Partly as a reaction to psychoanalytical approaches in the fifties, which were stigmatizing for mothers of autistic children, scientific research into the genetics and biology of autism took flight. For

---

1   Leo Kanner, 'Autistic Disturbances of Affective Contact', *Acta Paedopsychiatrica*, 35:4 (1968), 100–36, p. 249.

   https://doi.org/10.11647/OBP.0261.11

the last forty years, indeed, most autism research focused on its causes, often in the hope that some 'cure' might be found. Over the last decade, this has changed somewhat: many researchers no longer consider autism something to be cured. Still, autism is primarily conceived of as a phenomenon rooted in genetics. In what follows, we will explore the link between autism and genetics and the meaning of genetics. I will challenge the idea that biology and genetics are necessarily fixed, and argue that the gap between our biology or genetics and our experiences is not that wide.

Conceptualising the Causes of Autism

In chapter nine, we have seen, following Ian Hacking and Erving Goffman, that by giving someone a specific diagnosis, we also change their future and their past. They become an autistic person. Here is an example from our interview study. The person in question was a fifty-two-year-old woman who had just received her diagnosis a week before the interview. She states about the diagnosis: 'Yeah, I actually thought um... it's going to be a loss situation like um... if I don't have it, then it's because of my past, and it's a loss situation, and if I do have it, it's also a loss situation because I, I want to be able to communicate correctly.'[2] This lady had had a challenging childhood; her parents mistreated her. She had always wondered whether the problems she experienced with social contact were due to her problematic past or the fact that she was different. The diagnosis of autism as an innate and lifelong condition was proof that the latter was the case. Because of this, she also permitted herself to be kinder to herself. She continues:

> But I kind of already gave that up for a bit. I'm like, it will grow, uhm, but actually getting the diagnosis was a relief. I'm not putting myself down all the time anymore, yeah, and you can't, and... I don't blame myself as much anymore. I want to keep growing, and work on it. It's not that I give up like, I'll never be able to, no I want to be able to, but uhm, if I don't succeed, I no longer give myself a beating. I've actually become more relaxed... [3]

---

2   Kristien Hens and Raymond Langenberg, *Experiences of Adults Following an Autism Diagnosis* (Cham: Palgrave Macmillan, 2018).

3   Hens and Langenberg, *Experiences of Adults Following an Autism Diagnosis*, p. 86.

As we have already discussed, how we conceptualise autism and psychiatric disorders as more or less biological or genetic has ethical consequences. Although very little is known about the causes of psychiatric illness in general, empirical research has demonstrated that people think that different psychiatric diagnoses have different levels of innateness (versus acquiredness) and a psychological basis (versus a biological one).[4]

Delphine Jacobs is a child psychiatrist who researches how child psychiatrists and paediatricians view autism. As a PhD student, she investigated how the conceptualisation of autism as genetic and innate influenced how these clinical professionals looked at the prognosis and the possibility of improvement of symptoms. Clinicians who viewed autism as an innate and lifelong condition saw their clients' future as already fixed and less amenable to change, and often thought that children had less control about their behaviour than children diagnosed with ADHD. People with a diagnosis that is seen as innate, genetic, and biological are thought to be less responsible for their deeds than people with a personality disorder.[5] However, such conceptualisations also influence how people think about their responsibility towards people with a diagnosis. The more a specific phenomenon is seen as biological or innate, the more people think that medication is the best option to tackle the associated problems. Research also suggests that professionals may experience less empathy towards people with a diagnosis that they consider innate rather than psychological, although genetic explanations imply that these people would be less responsible for their deeds. Matthew Lebowitz and Woo-kyoung Ahn, the authors

---

4   Woo-kyoung Ahn and others, 'Beliefs about Essences and the Reality of Mental Disorders', *Psychological Science*, 17:9 (2006), 759–66, https://doi.org/10.1111/j.1467-9280.2006.01779.x; Woo-kyoung Ahn, Caroline C. Proctor, and Elizabeth H. Flanagan, 'Mental Health Clinicians' Beliefs About the Biological, Psychological, and Environmental Bases of Mental Disorders', *Cognitive Science*, 33:2 (2009), 147–82, https://doi.org/10.1111/j.1551-6709.2009.01008.x

5   Stephen Buetow and Glyn Elwyn, 'Are Patients Morally Responsible for Their Errors?', *Journal of Medical Ethics*, 32:5 (2006), 260–62, https://doi.org/10.1136/jme.2005.012245; Marc J. Miresco and Laurence J. Kirmayer, 'The Persistence of Mind-Brain Dualism in Psychiatric Reasoning about Clinical Scenarios', *The American Journal of Psychiatry*, 163:5 (2006), 913–18, https://doi.org/10.1176/ajp.2006.163.5.913

of these studies, suggest that this may be the case because these people are considered less 'human' and more controlled by their genes.[6]

In chapter two, we have discussed how psychiatric diagnoses are not 'like diabetes'. However, the more a diagnosis of autism is thought of as similar to diabetes, the more the person diagnosed has to accept it as an inescapable condition. This can lead to less importance being attributed to the content, meaning, and understanding of individual behaviours if people consider them to be explicable in mechanistic-biological terms. Think about specific interests of autistic people that are seen as examples of stereotypical behaviour. *For The Love of Dogs* is a documentary published on Aeon about a twelve-year-old boy diagnosed with Asperger syndrome, who has an extraordinary interest in and knowledge about dog breeds. The filmmakers follow him to a big dog show where he enthusiastically interacts with breeders and dogs. At a specific moment in the film, an autism specialist speaks: this type of specific interest, so she said, can be explained because for an autistic person, the outside world is chaotic and frightening, and these interests help them to structure their world: 'These children will use their particular narrow interests in order to reduce their anxiety'.[7] There may be some core of truth in this. However, at a certain point, the filmmakers decided to interview the dog owners at the show, not about autism, but about their love of dogs. All the other people at the dog show — probably without a diagnosis — shared the same level of interest: they also found comfort and support in their (interest in) dogs. Perhaps we can explain anyone's specific interests or hobbies by referring to a need for structure and support in a frightening world. An overly deterministic and fatalistic explanation can also be dangerous in clinical practice. Clinical psychologist Evi Verbeke describes two cases in which autism was presented to recently diagnosed people, adolescents in this case, as a medical diagnosis (such as diabetes) that one has to accept and that is lifelong, rather than as an explanation of and an answer to

---

6   Matthew S. Lebowitz and Woo-kyoung Ahn, 'Effects of Biological Explanations for Mental Disorders on Clinicians' Empathy', *Proceedings of the National Academy of Sciences of the United States of America*, 111:50 (2014), 17786–90, https://doi.org/10.1073/pnas.1414058111

7   *For the Love of Dogs*. Dir. Tim O'Donnell. Aeon. 16 min. 30 March 2015. https://aeon.co/videos/can-a-knowledge-of-dogs-help-a-boy-with-asperger-s-connect-with-people

the specific challenges that young people may experience at certain points in their lives. The diagnosis confronted these young people with existential questions about their own identity, which led to a worsening of their problems.[8]

Conceiving of autism as inherently genetic, innate, and lifelong can therefore also be problematic. Firstly, we only have limited knowledge about how autism develops throughout the lifespan, as there are only very few longitudinal studies that have been conducted. At the same time, the fact that autism is considered biologically real can help people with autism to accept their atypicality, limitations, and talents. Moreover, autism is real as a shared experience on a phenomenological level. Diagnosed people, their psychiatrists, and their peers will acknowledge that. Nevertheless, it would be wrong to mistake this phenomenological reality for a simple biological explanation, for example located in one gene or a specific part of the brain. This might lead us to consider autism simply as located in the individual and as static. However, we do not need genes or areas of the brain to acknowledge the reality of shared experiences. We might wonder if shared experiences are not 'more real' than genes or brain concepts. We may even ask ourselves to what extent genes themselves are real, and not merely linguistic representations of messy organic processes.[9]

The Meaning of Genes

As I have discussed in the previous chapter, we may have to consider more dynamic conceptions of biology, which require the study of experiences. I previously described the thoughts of one of the godfathers of a more dynamic approach to pathology, George Canguilhem. Now, I want to dig deeper into one of the most commonly researched and discussed themes when dealing with autism: the link with genetics.[10] Indeed, as Majia Nadesan has specified, the research

---

8   Evi Verbeke, 'Diagnoses als mogelijke decompenserende factor', *TIJDSCHRIFT VOOR PSYCHOANALYSE*, 22:4 (2016), 283–93.

9   John Dupré, *Processes of Life: Essays in the Philosophy of Biology* (Oxford: Oxford University Press, 2012).

10   Majia Holmer Nadesan, 'Autism and Genetics Profit, Risk, and Bare Life', in *Worlds of Autism: Across the Spectrum of Neurological Difference*, ed. by Joyce Davidson and Michael Orsini (Minneapolis: University of Minnesota Press, 2013), pp. 117–42.

into explanatory autism genes is like the quest for the holy grail. This emphasis on genetic causes can probably partly be explained by the power of biological and genetic explanations as such. In their book *The DNA Mystique*, Dorothy Nelkin and Susan Lindee describe this as follows:

> Introductory biology is presented as a valid, truth-seeking endeavour, untainted by religious, political, or philosophical commitments. It places human beings in a meaningful universe, providing ways of understanding relationships between ethnic and racial groups and between identity and the body. Biology, in a very real sense, has become a philosophical and religious domain, and the genome itself has become a guide to the human condition.[11]

After all, it is human to look for simple and understandable explanations of how one struggles. The authors describe how genetic essentialism has taken the place of earlier theistic explanations, but this can also be dangerous: genetic explanations remove individual and broader social responsibility.

The idea of autism as a genetic condition has always existed. Kanner and Asperger considered autism to be innate and saw similarities between parents and their children, although Kanner also acknowledged that there could be psychogenic causes. When the idea of the 'refrigerator mother' took root, parents welcomed genetic explanations. They saw these as proof that they were not 'guilty' and did not engender their child's autism. Autistic people sometimes use genetics to demonstrate that autism is a natural and neutral variant with advantages and disadvantages.[12] For some time, a distinction has been made between syndromic and idiopathic autism. In syndromic autism, autism is an expression of a genetic syndrome such as Fragile-X. Idiopathic autism is autism for which no genetic cause has been found. There is some hope that new insights concerning Copy Number Variants (CNVs) can blur this distinction. However, it is also possible that in the end, only common variants will be found, which are also present in the general

---

11   Dorothy Nelkin and M. Susan Lindee, *The DNA Mystique: The Gene as a Cultural Icon* (Ann Arbor: University of Michigan, 2004), p. xvii.

12   Pier Jaarsma and Stellan Welin, 'Autism as a Natural Human Variation: Reflections on the Claims of the Neurodiversity Movement', *Health Care Analysis*, 20:1 (2012), 20–30.

non-diagnosed population.[13] A great amount of research money has been poured into the search for the genetic origins of autism. Genetic researchers have associated almost every chromosome with autism, with moderate results. The fact that the vast majority of genetic findings are risk factors, not definite causes, raises the question why no more research is done into the environmental factors that are supposed to contribute to autism.

Genetics is one of the most researched topics in bioethics. Bioethics is a branch of philosophy that deals with the ethical implications of technological developments and research findings in biology and medicine. Specifically, many bioethicists research questions about the ethical implications of genetics. Should we screen embryos genetically, select or even modify embryos to make healthier children or even children in which certain characteristics such as intelligence are enhanced? For which diseases should prenatal genetic diagnosis and termination of pregnancy be allowed? What genetic information should be detected and communicated with people who are already born? We cannot answer these questions without thoroughly reflecting on the underlying concepts. What do we mean by 'disease'? Which risks are we allowed to take when we introduce new genetic technologies? What about the right not to know? What does responsibility mean? Do parents have the responsibility to choose the children with the most desirable characteristics, or should we accept future children as they are? If we look at autism through a genetic lens, such questions are no different from those asked about other conditions.

I researched the ethical aspects of genetic research and counselling in autism some years ago. I interviewed several Belgian psychiatrists, educational specialists, psychologists, and geneticists who dealt with autism daily. From my research, it became clear that these people had many questions about fundamental genetic research into autism.[14] Firstly, there is the question of who can participate in such research. A diagnosis of autism is a clinical diagnosis. People with the same

---

13 Kristien Hens, Hilde Peeters, and Kris Dierickx, 'The Ethics of Complexity. Genetics and Autism, a Literature Review', *American Journal of Medical Genetics Part B: Neuropsychiatric Genetics* (2016), https://doi.org/10.1002/ajmg.b.32432

14 Kristien Hens, Hilde Peeters, and Kris Dierickx, 'Shooting a Moving Target. Researching Autism Genes: An Interview Study with Professionals', *European Journal of Medical Genetics*, 59:1 (2016), 32–38, https://doi.org/10.1016/j.ejmg.2015.12.009

genetic characteristics do not necessarily all receive the same diagnosis, and people with the same diagnosis do not necessarily have the same underlying biological characteristics. People thought that the diagnosis itself was not sufficiently fine-grained to enable useful genetic research. Some were also concerned that genetic findings would pave the way towards a policy of prevention:

> We are giving an ambiguous message. On the one hand we say that it is not bad to have it, on the other hand we say it is better to prevent it. Especially for the people with ASD I believe that it is a kind of ethical dilemma, is it bad to have it or not. I doubt that geneticists ever wonder about this, but they should.[15]

> I am very ambiguous about this one. I am thinking, are we then going to develop drugs to make them all normal? I find that very difficult, because I do not believe in medication for that, especially not in developmental disorders.[16]

If we are talking about clinical genetic research in children or families in which, through psychiatric diagnostics, autism has been established, respondents often stress the power of genetics to remove blame or feelings of guilt.[17] Hence, the fact that a biological-genetic cause can be attributed enhances the deculpabilising effect of the diagnosis itself:

> The advantage of looking for a gene, it can mean a lot for these people if they are given a cause, or a reason why something goes wrong, a reassurance that it is not the way they raise the child, or because they have smoked or drank, the question of who is to blame. That is the positive side of the story. Except if you are dealing with a condition with an inherited susceptibility.[18]

Another advantage of finding a genetic cause for autism is that clinicians can explain to a family what is the risk that their next child will receive the same diagnosis. Here we enter rugged ethical terrain. We can ask whether autism is grounds for embryo selection, or prenatal

---

15   Hens, Peeters, and Dierickx, 'Shooting a Moving Target', p. 35.

16   Ibid.

17   Kristien Hens, Hilde Peeters, and Kris Dierickx, 'Genetic Testing and Counseling in the Case of an Autism Diagnosis: A Caregivers Perspective', *European Journal of Medical Genetics*, 59:9 (2016), 452–58, https://doi.org/10.1016/j.ejmg.2016.08.007

18   Hens, Peeters, and Dierickx, 'Genetic Testing and Counseling in the Case of an Autism Diagnosis', p. 454.

diagnostics and pregnancy termination, and who decides that. Majia Nadesan describes an autism genocide clock that was available online for some time:

> The possibility that gene-based susceptibility tests might be developed has raised considerable concern within particular subsets of the autism-advocacy movement. For example, for a time, there existed online an "autism genocide clock" that purported to count down years, days, and minutes to the seemingly inevitable developments of an autism prenatal test that would result in an autism holocaust. This clock was uploaded in 2001 in response to concerns that genetic knowledge about autism would lead to the patenting of susceptibility genes, which in turn could be used to develop commercial prenatal tests.[19]

Indeed, in 2018 a patent was approved for the development of diagnostic tests. This patent was based on a gene suspected of playing a role in the development of autism.[20] These diagnostic tests could not only identify a genetic cause in someone with a diagnosis of autism but could also reduce or even replace current diagnostic practices. Often, diagnosticians say that they would like to have clearer ways of diagnosing autism and prefer to have a more reliable diagnosis by using genetic markers. However, such an endeavour also has several challenges. Firstly, there is the fact that genetic factors are risk factors. Autism is a diagnosis given at the level of the phenotype based on behaviour. A diagnostic test based on genetics is, by definition, impossible within the current DSM-5 definition of autism. Furthermore, although a straightforwardly genetic and 'somatic' diagnosis of autism may seem to be more scientific than a behavioural diagnosis, as it would take away some uncertainty and avoid any element of guesswork, it would also bring new and complex challenges, some of which I have described earlier in the book. Collapsing psychiatric diagnosis with genetics may mean that experiences, which are also symptoms of autism, are neglected by caregivers. Behaviour that is directly explained by genetics may become more challenging to incorporate as part of one's identity. It is, however, precisely because autism is flexible and, at the same time, a shared

---

19   Majia Holmer Nadesan, *Constructing Autism: Unravelling the 'Truth' and Understanding the Social* (London; New York: Routledge, 2005), p. 125.

20   Kristien Hens and others, 'The Ethics of Patenting Autism Genes', *Nature Reviews. Genetics*, 19:5 (2018), 247–48, https://doi.org/10.1038/nrg.2018.17

experience that the diagnosis can work therapeutically. Moreover, there will always be people for whom no genetic 'cause' can be found, but for whom a diagnosis is still helpful.

Dynamic Genetics: The Strange Case of Epigenetics

Autism seems to be, to no small extent, familial, and a large amount of scientific resources are allocated to research into the identification of autism genes. Decades-long genetic research has, however, not provided a direct causal explanation for autism. It looks as if environmental factors play an essential role in the development of the autistic phenotype.[21] It is probably the interaction between genes and environment that can result in atypical development and the challenges that lead to a diagnosis of autism. There are probably also protective factors in the background that mean someone with a genetic susceptibility to develop autism may never receive the actual diagnosis. There have been many prenatal, perinatal, and postnatal factors associated with autism. Early socio-demographic factors such as income, education, and employment of the parents can influence the probability of a subsequent diagnosis.[22] Factors that influence the chance that people receive a diagnosis later in life have not been researched extensively.

Nevertheless, we can state that merely looking at genetic and neurological factors within the individual is not sufficient to predict that someone will get a diagnosis. The explanation of why research into environmental factors is still in its infancy has probably to do with the questionable and unscientific status of some of the earlier claims. On the one hand, the 'refrigerator mother' idea has led to problematic stigmatization of parents, specifically mothers. On the other hand, the faulty suggestion that a simple environmental factor such as vaccination may cause autism has also had far-reaching and disadvantageous effects.

---

21 William Mandy and Meng-Chuan Lai, 'Annual Research Review: The Role of the Environment in the Developmental Psychopathology of Autism Spectrum Condition', *Journal of Child Psychology and Psychiatry, and Allied Disciplines*, 57:3 (2016), 271–92, https://doi.org/10.1111/jcpp.12501

22 Jeffrey S. Karst and Amy Vaughan Van Hecke, 'Parent and Family Impact of Autism Spectrum Disorders: A Review and Proposed Model for Intervention Evaluation', *Clinical Child and Family Psychology Review*, 15:3 (2012), 247–77, https://doi.org/10.1007/s10567-012-0119-6

It may make more sense to look at genetics from a dynamic perspective. We do not look for one etiological explanation in early development, but we consider an individual as continuously in interaction with their environment. In what follows, I will explain epigenetics and how we can use this, as ethicists, to look differently at certain phenomena such as autism. What follows is a translation of a piece I wrote for the Dutch periodical *Karakter*.[23]

In a recent article in *Science*, Adam Klosin and colleagues describe how environmental factors influence gene expression and how these changes can be passed on to subsequent generations.[24] To examine this, they use a transgene C. elegans.[25] The roundworms were genetically modified to light up if they arrived in a warmer environment. If the worms were in an environment of twenty degrees Celsius, they glowed a little bit. When it became warmer, the gene that caused the fluorescence was switched on, and the worms started to glow more brightly. The fact that environmental factors influence gene expression is in itself not striking. When the temperature lowered again, the worms kept their intense glow. Furthermore, their descendants inherited the glow, and for seven subsequent generations, glowing worms were born. When C. elegans were kept in a warm environment for five generations, the glow characteristic was passed on to fourteen generations. This looks much like the inheritance of acquired characteristics as it was suggested by the French naturalist Jean-Baptiste Lamarck (1744–1829) but later discredited by Neo-Darwinism and modern genetics. It goes against what we call the 'central dogma' of genetics. This central dogma states that the transcription and translation of DNA to RNA and subsequently to proteins is one-way traffic. Inheritable changes in DNA, so people thought, can only happen by mutations in the genes themselves.

23 Kristien Hens, 'Dynamiek En Ethiek van de Epigenetica', *Karakter*, 2017, https://www.tijdschriftkarakter.be/dynamiek-en-ethiek-van-de-epigenetica/

24 Adam Klosin and others, 'Transgenerational Transmission of Environmental Information in C. Elegans', *Science*, 356.6335 (2017), 320–23, https://doi.org/10.1126/science.aah6412

25 C. elegans (Caenorhabditis elegans) is a roundworm that is 1 mm long and that is often used in genetic research, because the animal has a relatively simple genome and reproduces quickly so that generations quickly follow after another.

Of course, it has been known for a long time that this is not the whole story. The mechanism that is described above is known under the term 'epigenetics'. Skin cells and brain cells perform different functions. Hence, different genes must be expressed. Therefore, based on the environment in which the cell is found, there should be a mechanism that influences which genes express themselves and which do not. In 1911, Wilhelm Johanssen (1857–1927), who first named the distinction between genotype and phenotype, suggested that identical genotypes can produce different phenotypes. In 1942, Conrad Waddington (1905–1975) suggested using the term 'epigenetics' to describe the mechanisms involved in gene expression. 'Epi' is the Greek word for 'on, with'. In recent decades, the study of this epigenetic layer has taken off rapidly. One of the most studied mechanisms in this context is methylation, which occurs above the DNA level. If methyl groups (as small carbon compounds) are added or removed from specific regions, genes become accessible for transcriptions. Techniques such as Genome-Wide Methylation Analysis allow for the study of methylation patterns.

Epigenetics is extremely interesting for bioethicists who are reflecting on genetics. Often, in discussions about the impact of genetics, the unidirectional model promoted by the 'central dogma' is assumed. Genes may be edited through CRISPR/Cas9, or embryos can be selected based on the 'best' genotype. Bioethicists sometimes think about the influence of environmental factors, for example, in discussions about the extent to which we can force pregnant women to have a healthy lifestyle. These environmental factors are often perceived as secondary because they are considered changeable. Recent epigenetics findings suggest the molecular link between our genetic blueprint and the environment, between nature and nurture.

Moreover, epigenetic changes resonate for a long time, even after the individual has moved on from their earlier environment. It is likely that specific changes are also passed on to future generations. Techniques such as CRISPR/Cas9 that allow us to change pieces of DNA directly are somewhat invasive. Targeted manipulation of the layer above the DNA is perhaps a much easier way to decide which genes can be expressed and which cannot. In this way, specific epigenetic changes could be undone, a method that is being investigated in research carried out into certain cancers.

All these aspects of epigenetics (inheritance, reversibility, molecular linking of environmental factors) influence how we think about responsibility. Who is responsible for the impact of societal change on individuals and vice versa? It has been demonstrated that pollution through particulate matter can induce epigenetic changes, with potentially severe consequences for the health of children yet to be born. However, we might wonder who or what causes the fact that many people can only afford to live close to the highway or in polluted areas. Moreover, even if people move out of polluted areas, will the molecular changes still affect future generations? It is self-evident that parents are responsible for their children's health, but the question is how far they can control certain factors themselves.

An intermediate conclusion could be that our level of responsibility is disproportionately inflated if we take the implications of epigenetics seriously. The fact that living close to the highway is not healthy is common knowledge. The idea that breathing in particulate matter can resonate on a molecular level, and that harm has already been done by the time we determine the levels of pollution, can lead to an unbearable sense of guilt on the one hand or moral defeatism on the other. If we read scientific literature about epigenetics, we do indeed find terminology that implies blame and responsibility. In 2005, Marcus Pembrey and his colleagues found that when boys start to smoke at a young age, this affects the BMI of their sons born later in life.[26] A commentary on this phenomenon in *Nature* is titled 'The sins of the fathers and their fathers'.[27] Again in *Nature,* Richardson and her colleagues warned in 2014 how reporting epigenetic findings can lead to pregnant women becoming overburdened with guilt: they would be held responsible for epigenetic changes during pregnancy.[28] Indeed, a couple of years ago, newspaper headlines reported on findings that eating an English breakfast (particularly bacon and eggs) at the beginning of pregnancy could increase the intelligence of the future child.[29]

---

26 Marcus E Pembrey and others, 'Sex-Specific, Male-Line Transgenerational Responses in Humans', *Eur J Hum Genet*, 14:2 (2005), 159–66.

27 Emma Whitelaw, 'Epigenetics: Sins of the Fathers, and Their Fathers', *European Journal of Human Genetics*, 14:2 (2006), 131–32, https://doi.org/10.1038/sj.ejhg.5201567

28 Sarah S. Richardson and others, 'Society: Don't Blame the Mothers', *Nature*, 512:7513 (2014), 131–32, https://doi.org/10.1038/512131a

29 Sarah Young, 'Eating Fry-Ups During Pregnancy Can Boost Babies' Intelligence, Research Indicates', *The Independent*, 7 January 2018, https://www.independent.co.uk/life-style/pregnant-women-eat-fry-up-bacon-eggs-intelligence-babies-choline-a8146216.html

Ethicists may wonder if mothers have a duty to ensure that their offspring are as bright as possible. The environment in utero seems to be susceptible to epigenetic influences. Mothers, who traditionally already bear the most significant responsibility for their baby's welfare, risk also being held responsible for their child's future health and that of these children's future children. Research in mice has demonstrated that stress during pregnancy influences the BMI of offspring and can also lead to hyperactive behaviour in offspring. However, this finding does not automatically lead to the conclusion that women must give up a stressful job during the entire pregnancy. Perhaps the emphasis in the media on scientific research into environmental factors in utero is unbalanced. Other factors, for example, the impact of the quality of the sperm of the biological father, might be neglected too often. People frequently forget that environmental factors do not only exert influence during pregnancy. As already mentioned, epigenetic changes in the primordial germ cell of teenage boys, caused by activities such as smoking or drinking, can be passed to the sperm cells they produce. These changes are cumulative during a lifetime. That it is better not to smoke or drink as a teenager is self-evident.

The idea that fifteen-year-old boys could be persuaded not to do this out of a sense of duty towards the health of their future children and grandchildren might be a stretch too far. We must avoid a kind of epigenetic determinism, where we replace a single genetic explanation with a simplistic epigenetic explanation. Such substitution will lead to an unwarranted emphasis being placed on individual responsibilities. If we take epigenetics seriously, we must adopt a complex and dynamic view of organisms, acknowledging the multicausal nature of behaviour. We must also take seriously the impact of experiences on biology, which is often outside of our control. Such a systemic view of the functioning of organisms suggests that epigenetics ought to play a role in the decisions of policymakers. It is, among other things, a wake-up call that the pernicious effects of environmental pollution have systemic and long-lasting effects and need a systemic solution.

The fact that researchers have found such a molecular link between nature and nurture will undoubtedly influence how we see ourselves as human beings in relation to our environment; The image of the human being as built up from a genetic blueprint, only fleetingly influenced by our milieu, is being challenged. Human organisms become dynamic entities in interaction with the environment on a molecular level. This thought is, of course, not new. As I have previously described, Canguilhem and others presented more systemic approaches to human life. Nowadays, Developmental Systems Theory scholars, drawing on findings in epigenetics, defend the idea that human nature is the result of the entire organic milieu in which development takes place, challenging the primacy of genetics. A human being is not something atomistic or universal. As such, we come close here to the concept of epigenesis.

Epigenesis is at first only tangentially related to epigenetics. It ties into a century-old discussion relating to the form of organisms. Epigenesis means that an organism's form is not wholly predetermined from the start (as preformationists would say). It is shaped by influences from inside of an organism: for example, the location of a cell in the body influences the function it performs, but so do external influences. In this sense, an epigenetic approach is a developmental approach: organisms are always in development, not solely when they are young. Their nature and functioning are thoroughly influenced by what they experience on their path through life. Hence, modern-day epigenetics could be seen as a vindication of the age-old concept of epigenesis.

Such a developmental approach to what it means to be human also has ethical implications. Autism might be a good example of this. After decades of research into its genetic origins, a consensus is growing that environmental factors and epigenetics play a role. Moreover, autism is heterogeneous and complex, referring to a wide array of cognitive functioning and behaviour that is variable across a lifetime and has a varying influence on wellbeing. Autism is, in the first place, a behavioural diagnosis that is attributed according to DSM-5 guidelines. Simultaneously, autistic people sometimes argue that it is not a condition or disease, but a neutral genetic variant that needs to be accepted and accommodated. Furthermore, epigenetic findings suggest that autism is a genetic adaptation that could be triggered by changes in the environment.

Nevertheless, I am convinced that the emphasis that people sometimes now put on unhealthy environmental factors and lifestyle as a cause of autism, through which it is suggested that autism is due to something that has gone wrong or something that could be avoided, is misguided and may even be an example of the epigenetic determinism described above. On the contrary, an epigenetic view of organisms demonstrates that searching for simple causes of certain behaviours is naive.

We might consider whether there is something like 'epigenetic normality', a baseline from which we can measure deviations. In a seminal paper, Charles Dupras and Vardit Ravitsky ask this question. They give the example of obesity, which is associated with malnourishment during pregnancy: the foetus reacts to this with epigenetic changes that allow for more efficient storage of nutrients.[30] If the child subsequently grows up in normal circumstances, there is an increased likelihood of obesity. Perhaps similar mechanisms are at work in autism. This might support the argument that the challenges and suffering of some autistic people are due as much to the broader environment in which they are situated as their neurological atypicality. As already demonstrated in the context of environmental factors and the responsibility of the pregnant mother, it would be incorrect to replace one explanatory model (the genetic one) with another (a specific environmental factor). Dysfunctioning and functioning are the results of complex interactions, of which we may only know the tip of the iceberg and which are not solely located within the individual. When we appreciate the impact of epigenetics fully, we can assume that there is a molecular basis for a complex, systemic, and plastic concept of human beings, which dynamically change their environment and are being changed by it. This concept is moreover ethically relevant to the aims and methods of medicine. We can question biomedical research that merely seeks to discover the one cause of autism in genes or specific environmental factors. It makes more sense to encourage approaches that consider the autistic person and the challenges they may experience in a particular context, and consider how they cope and can cope with this context. In this way, we can fully appreciate autism as a developmental phenomenon.

---

30   Charles Dupras and Vardit Ravitsky, 'The Ambiguous Nature of Epigenetic Responsibility', *Journal of Medical Ethics*, 42:8 (2016), 534–41, https://doi.org/10.1136/medethics-2015-103295

Epilogue

Towards an Ethics of Autism

In April 2018, I led a workshop for educational scientists, psychologists, and child psychiatrists who were autism experts. I started this workshop by lecturing about certain concepts, such as the looping effects of Ian Hacking, and by asking questions related to the ontological status of autism. Subsequently, I interacted with the participants: I asked them how psychiatric diagnoses are different from somatic diagnoses. After that, I presented our phenomenological study with autistic adults. We also discussed some of the ethical questions that participants had sent me beforehand. Such questions included the following: What to do with an adolescent who refuses a diagnosis? Can we force them to take on and accept the diagnosis, as you would if an adolescent refused a diagnosis of diabetes? Who is best to inform a child about her diagnosis—autism professionals or the parents? What if, primarily, the parents want a diagnosis because they are looking for an explanation for specific challenges they face, but the child herself is doing well? A recurring question in many discussions about autism is how to explain the diagnosis. Autism professionals ask themselves how they should respond to the fact that descriptions that represent autism as something inherent in the brain, such as the idea that neurons in autistic brains are hyperconnected, actually help people understand their diagnosis. Such explanations are not completely established as universal scientific facts but help the person who is confronted with specific challenges. Autism is conceived as real if one suspects a biological cause. It means that the person in question is no longer merely unwilling to cooperate, or bothersome. The clinical professionals in the workshop asked me whether it would be acceptable to use such brain analogies, even if they

     https://doi.org/10.11647/OBP.0261.12

are just that, analogies. This may imply tweaking the truth a bit in order to give their clients the clarity they seek.

From the literature and bioethical discussions about autism, we know that, as well as these questions clinicians may have, there are other issues regarding autism. Is autism something we should cure or prevent? Can we develop prenatal tests to detect autism in unborn foetuses? Do we have a duty to adapt society so that autistic people can feel at home? Perhaps autism is an invention of language, a social construct, and we should do away with a diagnosis, as some have suggested. We have arrived at the end of this book about the dynamics and ethics of autism. Those who expect a ready-made answer to these clinical and bioethical questions come home empty-handed. Rather than answering ethical questions, we have described different ways we might look at autism. To arrive at such a framework, we had to make a long journey. We saw that autism is a layered and polysemous concept and that it is perhaps senseless to try to bring back autism to a single biological or cognitive explanatory model.

In chapter one, I demonstrated that the ambiguities of the meaning of autism are already present in the descriptions by the two alleged founding fathers of autism, Leo Kanner and Hans Asperger. Leo Kanner described autism as a childhood developmental disorder. In his first paper, he assumed that autism is something innate but that the affected children do evolve after a period of time to have more social contact. Hans Asperger considered autism to be a personality disorder, lifelong, and with positive and negative sides—although in discussions of Asperger syndrome, scholars mostly talk about it being a developmental disorder. Today, people regard autism as an intrinsic property of a person, a certain way of thinking or feeling with which one is born and dies. Autism, or Autism Spectrum Disorder, is also a psychiatric diagnosis that a multidisciplinary team attributes to someone. Besides certain behavioural characteristics, this team determines whether the person suffers from these characteristics or whether they affect daily functioning. Indeed, it is not sufficient to have certain characteristics; these characteristics have to lead to certain types of challenges.

In chapter two, we tackled the question of what psychiatric diagnoses are. We investigated what it means for a phenomenon to be considered a mental disorder. Taking Nomy Arpaly's paper as a starting point,

I described how it is wrong to think that psychiatric diagnoses are merely somatic diagnoses of which we have yet to discover the cause. Psychiatric diagnoses have content; they are about something. If we neglect that content in favour of mere etiological description, we are making a mistake. We also investigated the extent to which categories in the DSM correspond to real, underlying biological essences. I described how psychiatric diagnoses are collections of behaviours that often co-occur but for which we have not necessarily found a single biological cause. Nevertheless, a definition in the DSM often also leads to reification. Reification is the idea that there must be some biological essence underneath. This does not imply that we can unmask categories such as autism as being unscientific and not real. It still is the case that a diagnosis of autism often corresponds to an experience shared by the clinician and the person diagnosed.

In chapter three, we discussed the main cognitive explanatory models of autism. We tackled the question of how people have tried to explain the behaviours associated with autism. I used one example, that of a deficient Theory of Mind, to demonstrate how scholars in meta-ethics have often used autism to test the validity of certain moral theories. A lesson we drew from this is that we have to test the extent to which explanatory models correspond to the experiences of autistic people. Autistic people have criticized the deficient ToM model because they do often do not recognize themselves in the description. Moreover, sometimes this has engendered the idea that autistic people are less human. Non-autistic people often have similar difficulties with understanding autistic people's minds. In chapter four, I dealt with sociological explanatory models of autism. We investigated how, in recent decades, the diagnosis of autism has expanded greatly and how this is not merely due to new scientific insights. Some scholars have described the specific circumstances in which the diagnosis of autism has come to exist. For example, they describe how children with an intellectual disability were no longer automatically sent to institutions in the second half of the twentieth century. Subsequently, their parents actively sought solutions and treatments for their children, whom they now raised at home. They often found these solutions in therapies available for autism. The discovery of the Broader Autism Phenotype made it possible for us to identify people exhibiting less striking autistic features in the context of autism. Moreover, the advent of child psychology and child psychiatry led to children becoming the subjects of psychological measurements and discussions about typical development.

In chapter five, I discussed different models of disability. Is disability, as bioethical discourse often presumes, by definition something we should avoid? Is it merely located in the individual? Certain models of disability, such as the social model, will claim that disability arises from social institutions, behaviours, and practices that make life difficult for people with certain bodily or cognitive characteristics. It is therefore important to change the context rather than cure the individual. However, a model that emphasises institutions and the environment could also neglect the individual experiences of a person with an atypical body or brain. Crip Theory tries to look at the different narratives of disability in a polysemous way and encourages us to take the stories of people with a disability seriously.

Chapter six then asks why it has been the case that researchers have not always taken the stories of autistic people seriously. For a long time, some scholars assumed that autistic people had a diminished sense of self, and therefore researchers did not take their accounts seriously. I analysed this as a form of epistemic injustice. We are doing an injustice to autistic people if we do not listen to their stories, and if we see them as less reliable narrators. I also described here the problems that can arise if preferences about communication differ. Suppose we consider it our moral duty to engage with autistic people. In that case, it is also our moral duty to look for ways to include those who use different communication methods or those who have an intellectual disability. Chapter seven sketched some of the conclusions of the interview study that Raymond Langenberg and I did with adults with a recent diagnosis of autism. We described how autistic people still dynamically interacted with their environment, although people often see them as inflexible. By having conversations and by double-checking their experiences with others, they understood themselves better. In chapter eight, I reflected, by way of interlude, on autism and time, and what it means to have a different sense of time.

In chapter nine, we returned to questions about the nature of psychiatric diagnoses. Using ideas from labelling theory and Ian Hacking's looping effects, I clarified how diagnostic labels influence how people look at themselves and how the environment looks at them. Both classified persons and the diagnostic criteria change during this process. The concept of autism and the group classified as autistic people are, therefore, always changing. In chapter ten, I continued to describe dynamic models of biology itself. Based on the previous discussions, I do not consider it desirable to conclude that autism does not exist or that it is purely in someone's mind. Autistic people share experiences, and these shared experiences are real and give meaning to autism. Moreover, a strict division between mental and somatic phenomena is hard to maintain, and looking at autism as a fundamentally biological condition also has certain advantages. People testify that they feel relieved from blame by a diagnosis, enabling them to let go of their perfectionism. This is also the case for the parents of autistic children. Nevertheless, thinking about a condition as something biological or genetic also has certain disadvantages. People often consider a biological cause to be static and unchangeable, and something one has simply to accept. I use the ideas of Georges Canguilhem to demonstrate that it is also possible to think about biology and pathology more dynamically and interactively. Enactivism achieves this for the human mind. Furthermore, Karen Barad's new materialism demonstrates that materialism does not necessarily have to be synonymous with reductionism and determinism.

Chapter eleven zoomed in on the relationship between autism and genetics. Since the first descriptions of autism, there has been a tension between autism as something innate and genetic, and autism as psychogenic. The former approach has become dominant in most countries. As a result, there has been a proliferation of genetic studies into the causes of autism. Conceptualising autism as genetic has certain advantages: even more than the diagnostic label alone, the fact that autism is seen as a genetic phenomenon works to relieve people from blame. Because of our prejudices regarding genetics, autism may be considered a problem located in the individual, which must be prevented or cured. In this chapter, I used epigenetics as an example of a more dynamic view of human biology, and I sketched the possibilities of this approach in the context of autism. Such dynamic approaches may lead to the search for simplistic etiological explanations for autism being given less weight. There is more space for considering an individual in her context and at a certain point in her life. The importance of an individual's own experience can then become an integral part of clinical care and scientific research. In this way, we can look at autism as a truly epigenetic or developmental phenomenon, which is inherently connected with the contexts and circumstances people encounter on their life path.

Such an approach may help us to tackle specific clinical-ethical dilemmas. Let us go back to the questions that were raised by the participants of the workshop I mentioned above, regarding diagnosis in children and adolescents. Often, clinicians state that it is of the utmost importance that autism is detected early to prevent specific problems later on. Autism is then presented as a reality to be discovered, like diabetes. It is striking that it is often not specified what exactly is discovered, as at a very early age there is often no dysfunctioning. It is often also unclear which problems people want to (or can) prevent. Are we talking about learning how to support the child better? Do we want to encourage their development towards a more typical path, if that is even possible? For many autistic people, the prevention of autism is not a worthwhile goal. They consider their specific way of being to be inextricably linked to their identity. Nevertheless, of course, some children can indeed suffer from specific characteristics that are associated with autism. Preventing suffering seems to be a good aim.

When talking about diagnoses and tests in childhood, we often refer to the child's right to an open future, a principle that was first laid down by Joel Feinberg, a philosopher of law.[1] Children are becoming gradually more autonomous as they grow older: we should not make decisions that would impair children's future autonomy unless this has immediate benefits for the child. For example, ethicists often assume that parents do not have the right to know specific genetic facts about their child if that knowledge is not immediately practical. Children should be allowed to decide for themselves what information they want to know and what they do not. Parents can find out about genetic conditions that require preventive intervention from an early age onwards. How does this translate to diagnostics? At first sight, a diagnosis opens up certain opportunities for the child that they would otherwise miss. A diagnosis can improve the relationship between

---

1   Joel Feinberg, 'The Child's Right to an Open Future', in *Philosophy of Education: An Anthology*, ed. by Randall R. Curren (Hoboken: Blackwell, 2007).

parent and child and give parents guidelines on how to raise their child. Still, it may also be that something is taken away from a child by giving a diagnosis: if we interpret autism as a lifelong condition, it means that the child does not have any choice other than to accept autism as an intricate part of her identity. But we have discussed how a psychiatric diagnosis is not only a mere description of a disorder in the individual. Such a diagnosis must actively be incorporated into one's own identity. Is that something we can decide for the child? What if an adolescent decides not to see herself as autistic anymore? Do we have to force her to accept the diagnosis at all costs?

This is not a plea for or against early diagnosis. We cannot predict the future. I think that a contextual, dynamic approach can offer some relief here. A diagnosis of autism can help parents and their children. It can lead to a better understanding of specific challenges. We must consider these challenges in the specific context and milieu of the individual. Whether a young adolescent who no longer views certain cognitive peculiarities as a limitation should consider herself as autistic or not must be discussed with them at an appropriate time. For some, autism will be an inextricable identity. Others will identify differently. Therefore, it is important to continue talking to clients about their relationship to their challenges and their diagnosis, and not to view diagnosis as a singular event, but as something that can be dynamically renegotiated. I want to refer back to Karl Jaspers here: Jaspers advocated for a phenomenological-hermeneutic approach to psychiatry. This entails an empathic understanding of the other, and requires us to look at problems from different perspectives, including biological perspectives. We should not consider autism as static and deterministic, but we should look at all levels of functioning as dynamic and context-sensitive. If we take autism seriously as a developmental phenomenon, this means acknowledging the many meanings it can have, and appreciating the relevance of the person's experiences throughout their lifetime, including in relation to the diagnosis itself.

Bibliography

Adriaens, Pieter R. and Andreas De Block, 'Why We Essentialize Mental Disorders', *The Journal of Medicine and Philosophy: A Forum for Bioethics and Philosophy of Medicine*, 38, 2 (2013), 107–27, https://doi.org/10.1093/jmp/jht008

Ahn, Woo-kyoung, Caroline C. Proctor, and Elizabeth H. Flanagan, 'Mental Health Clinicians' Beliefs About the Biological, Psychological, and Environmental Bases of Mental Disorders', *Cognitive Science*, 33, 2 (2009), 147–82, https://doi.org/10.1111/j.1551-6709.2009.01008.x

Ahn, Woo-kyoung, Elizabeth H. Flanagan, Jessecae K. Marsh, and Charles A. Sanislow, 'Beliefs About Essences and the Reality of Mental Disorders', *Psychological Science*, 17 (2006), 759–66, https://doi.org/10.1111/j.1467-9280.2006.01779.x

Alaimo, Stacy and Susan Hekman, *Material Feminisms* (Bloomington: Indiana University Press, 2008).

American Psychiatric Association, *Diagnostic and Statistical Manual of Mental Disorders*, 5th edition (Arlington: American Psychiatric Publishing, 2013).

Arpaly, Nomy, 'How It Is Not "Just Like Diabetes": Mental Disorders and the Moral Psychologist', *Philosophical Issues*, 15 (2005), 282–98, https://doi.org/10.1111/j.1533-6077.2005.00067.x

Asperger, Hans, 'Die „Autistischen Psychopathen" im Kindesalter', *Archiv für Psychiatrie und Nervenkrankheiten*, 117 (1944), 76–136.

Barad, Karen, *Meeting the Universe Halfway: Quantum Physics and the Entanglement of Matter* (Durham, NC: Duke University Press, 2007).

Bargiela, Sarah, Robyn Steward, and William Mandy, 'The Experiences of Late-Diagnosed Women with Autism Spectrum Conditions: An Investigation of the Female Autism Phenotype', *Journal of Autism and Developmental Disorders*, 46 (2016), 3281–94, https://doi.org/10.1007/s10803-016-2872-8

Barnbaum, Deborah R., *The Ethics of Autism: Among Them, but Not of Them* (Bloomington: Indiana University Press, 2008).

Barnes, Elizabeth, *The Minority Body: A Theory of Disability* (Oxford: Oxford University Press, 2016).

Baron-Cohen, Simon, 'Two New Theories of Autism: Hyper-systemising and Assortative Mating', *Archives of Disease in Childhood*, 91 (2006), 2–5, http://doi.org/10.1136/adc.2005.075846

Baron-Cohen, Simon, Alan M. Leslie, and Uta Frith, 'Does the Autistic Child Have a "Theory of Mind"?', *Cognition*, 21 (1985), 37–46, https://doi.org/10.1016/0010-0277(85)90022-8

Baron-Cohen, Simon, 'Editorial Perspective: Neurodiversity – a Revolutionary Concept for Autism and Psychiatry', *Journal of Child Psychology and Psychiatry*, 58, 6 (2017), 744–47, https://doi.org/10.1111/jcpp.12703

Baron-Cohen, Simon, 'Is Asperger Syndrome/High-Functioning Autism necessarily a Disability?', *Development and Psychopathology*, 12, 3 (2000), 489–500, https://doi.org/10.1017/S0954579400003126

Baron-Cohen, Simon, 'The Extreme Male Brain Theory of Autism', *Trends in Cognitive Sciences*, 6, 6 (2002), 248–54, https://doi.org/10.1016/s1364-6613(02)01904-6

Baron-Cohen, Simon, *Mindblindness: An Essay on Autism and Theory of Mind* (Cambridge, MA: MIT Press, 1997).

Benham, Jessica L. and James S. Kizer, 'Aut-Ors of Our Experience: Interrogating Intersections of Autistic Identity', *Canadian Journal of Disability Studies*, 5, 3 (2016), 77–113, http://dx.doi.org/10.15353/cjds.v5i3.298

Bettelheim, Bruno, *The Empty Fortress: Infantile Autism and the Birth of the Self*, New edition edition (Illinois: Free Press, 1972).

Block, Andreas De and Pieter Adriaens, *Born this way: een filosofische blik op wetenschap en homoseksualiteit* (Belgium: LannooCampus, 2015).

Boorse, Christopher, 'Health as a Theoretical Concept', *Philosophy of Science*, 44, 4 (1977), 542–73, https://doi.org/10.1086/288768

Boroditsky, Lera, 'How Languages Construct Time', in *Space, Time and Number in the Brain*, ed. by Stanislas Dehaene and Elizabeth Brannon (Oxford: Oxford University Press, 2011), pp. 333–41.

Borsboom, Denny, Gideon J. Mellenbergh, and Jaap van Heerden, 'The Concept of Validity', *Psychological Review*, 111, 4 (2004), 1061–71, https://doi.org/10.1037/0033-295x.111.4.1061

Bosman, Anna M. T., 'Disorders Are Reduced Normativity Emerging from the Relationship Between Organisms and Their Environment' in *Parental Responsibility in the Context of Neuroscience and Genetics*, ed. by Kristien Hens, Daniela Cutas and Dorothee **Horstkötter**, International Library of Ethics, Law, and the New Medicine series, 69 (Chambersburg: Springer International Publishing, 2017), pp. 35–54, https://doi.org/10.1007/978-3-319-42834-5

Buetow, Stephen and Glyn Elwyn, 'Are Patients Morally Responsible for Their Errors?', *Journal of Medical Ethics*, 32, 5 (2006), 260–62, https://doi.org/10.1136/jme.2005.012245

Canguilhem, Georges, *The Normal and the Pathological* (New York: Zone Books, 1989).

Chapman, Robert, 'Neurodiversity, Disability, Wellbeing' in *Neurodiversity Studies: A New Critical Paradigm*, ed. by Nick Chown, Anna Stenning and Hanna Rosquvist (Abingdon: Routledge: 2020).

Chapman, Robert, 'The Reality of Autism: On the metaphysics of disorder and diversity', *Philosophical Psychology*, 33, 6 (2019), 799–819, https://doi.org/10.1080/09515089.2020.1751103

Chapman, Robert, 'Neurodiversity Theory and its Discontents: Autism, Schizophrenia, and the Social Model' in *The Bloomsbury Companion to the Philosophy of Psychiatry*, ed. by Serife Tekin and Robyn Bluhm (London: Bloomsbury Academic, 2019).

Craig, Francesco, Francesco Margari, Anna R Legrottaglie, Roberto Palumbi, Concetta de Giambattista, and Lucia Margari, 'A Review of Executive Function Deficits in Autism Spectrum Disorder and Attention-Deficit/ Hyperactivity Disorder', *Neuropsychiatric Disease and Treatment*, 12 (2016), 1191–202, https://doi.org/10.2147/ndt.s104620

Crespi, Bernard J., 'Revisiting Bleuler: Relationship between Autism and Schizophrenia', *The British Journal of Psychiatry*, 196, 6 (2010), 495–95, https://doi.org/10.1192/bjp.196.6.495

Czech, Herwig, 'Hans Asperger, National Socialism, and "Race Hygiene" in Nazi-Era Vienna', *Molecular Autism*, 9 (2018), 29, https://doi.org/10.1186/s13229-018-0208-6

De Jaegher, Hanne, 'Embodiment and Sense-Making in Autism', *Frontiers in Integrative Neuroscience*, 7 (2013), https://doi.org/10.3389/fnint.2013.00015

Dehue, Trudy, *Betere mensen: over gezondheid als keuze en koopwaar* (Amsterdam: Atlas Contact, Uitgeverij, 2014).

Dehue, Trudy, *De depressie-epidemie: over de plicht het lot in eigen hand te nemen* (Amsterdam: Atlas Contact, Uitgeverij, 2015).

Descartes, René, *Discours de la méthode* (Collection Résurgences, 1995).

Deschrijver, Elaine and Colin Palmer, 'Reframing social cognition: Relational versus representational mentalizing', *Psychological Bulletin*, 146, 11 (2020), 941–69, https://doi.org/10.1037/bul0000302

DeVidi, David, 'Advocacy, Autism and Autonomy' in *The Philosophy of Autism*, ed. by Jami L. Anderson and Simon Cushing (Lanham: Rowman & Littlefield, 2013), pp. 187–200.

Dick, Philip K., *Martian Time-Slip* (New York: Vintage Books, 1964).

Dilthey, Wilhelm, 'Entwürfe Zur Kritik Der Historischen Vernunft Erster Teil: Erleben, Ausdruck Und Verstehen' in *Der Aufbau Der Geschichtlichen Welt in*

Den Geisteswissenschaften, Wilhelm Dilthey. Gesammelte Schriften, Volume 7 (Göttingen: Vandenhoeck & Ruprecht, 1992), pp. 191–251.

Dilthey, Wilhelm, 'Ideen Über Eine Beschreibende Und Zergliedernde Psychologie (1894)' in *Die Geistige Welt,* Wilhelm Dilthey. Gesammelte Schriften, Volume 5, 0 vols (Göttingen: Vandenhoeck & Ruprecht, 1990), pp. 139–240.

Drenth, Annemieke Van, 'Rethinking the Origins of Autism: Ida Frye and the Unraveling of Children's Inner World in the Netherlands in the Late 1930s', *Journal of the History of the Behavioural Sciences,* 54 (2018), 25–42, https://doi.org/10.1002/jhbs.21884

Dupras, Charles and Vardit Ravitsky, 'The Ambiguous Nature of Epigenetic Responsibility', *Journal of Medical Ethics,* 42 (2016), 534–41, http://doi.org/10.1136/medethics-2015-103295

Dupré, John, *Processes of Life: Essays in the Philosophy of Biology* (Oxford: Oxford University Press, 2012).

Evans, Bonnie, *The Metamorphosis of Autism: A History of Child Development in Britain* (Manchester: Manchester University Press, 2017).

Eyal, Gil, 'For a Sociology of Expertise: The Social Origins of the Autism Epidemic', *American Journal of Sociology,* 118, 4 (2013), 863–907, https://doi.org/10.7916/D8H70F1X

Eyal, Gil, ed., *The Autism Matrix: The Social Origins of the Autism Epidemic* (Cambridge, UK ; Malden, MA: Polity, 2010).

Faulkner, William, *The Sound and the Fury* (New York: Knopf Doubleday Publishing Group, 1984)

Feinberg, Joel, 'The Child's Right to an Open Future' in *Philosophy of Education: An Anthology,* ed. by Randall R. Curren (Oxford: Blackwell, 2007).

Fenton, Andrew and Tim Krahn, 'Autism, Neurodiversity, and Equality beyond the "Normal"', *Journal of Ethics in Mental Health,* 2 (2007).

Foucault, Michel, *Geschiedenis van de waanzin in de zeventiende en achttiende eeuw* (Amsterdam: Boom, 1982).

Fricker, Miranda, *Epistemic Injustice: Power and the Ethics of Knowing: Power and the Ethics of Knowing* (Oxford: Clarendon Press, 2007).

Frith, Uta and Francesca Happé, 'Theory of Mind and Self-Consciousness: What Is It Like to Be Autistic?', *Mind and Language,* 14 (1999), 1–22, https://doi.org/10.1111/1468-0017.00100

Frith, Uta, *Autism: Explaining the Enigma,* 2nd ed. (Malden, MA: Blackwell Publishing, 2003).

Fuchs, Thomas and Hanne De Jaegher, 'Enactive Intersubjectivity: Participatory Sense-Making and Mutual Incorporation', *Phenomenology and the Cognitive Sciences,* 8, 4 (2009), 465–86, https://doi.org/10.1007/s11097-009-9136-4

Fuchs, Thomas and Zeno Van Duppen, 'Time and Events: On the Phenomenology of Temporal Experience in Schizophrenia (Ancillary Article to EAWE Domain 2)', *Psychopathology*, 50 (2017), 68–74, https://doi.org/10.1159/000452768

Gabriel, Markus, *I Am Not a Brain: Philosophy of Mind for the 21st Century* (Hoboken: Wiley, 2017).

Gallagher, Shaun, 'Understanding Interpersonal Problems in Autism: Interaction Theory As an Alternative to Theory of Mind', *Philosophy, Psychiatry, and Psychology*, 11, 3 (2004), http://doi.org/10.1353/ppp.2004.0063

Ghaemi, S. Nassir, *The Rise and Fall of the Biopsychosocial Model: Reconciling Art and Science in Psychiatry* (Baltimore: JHU Press, 2010).

Gomez, Camilo R., 'Time Is Brain: The Stroke Theory of Relativity', *Journal of Stroke and Cerebrovascular Diseases: The Official Journal of National Stroke Association*, 27, 8 (2018), 2214–27, https://doi.org/10.1016/j.jstrokecerebrovasdis.2018.04.001

Gonzalez-Barrero, Ana Maria, and Aparna S. Nadig, 'Can Bilingualism Mitigate Set-Shifting Difficulties in Children With Autism Spectrum Disorders?', *Child Development*, 90, 4 (2017), 1043–60, https://doi.org/10.1111/cdev.12979

Goodley, Dan and Katherine Runswick-Cole, 'Reading Rosie: The Postmodern Dis/Abled Child', *Educational and Child Psychology*, 29, 2 (2012), 53-66.

Griffiths, Paul E., 'Our Plastic Nature' in *Transformations of Lamarckism: From Subtle Fluids to Molecular Biology*, ed. by Snait Gissis and Eva Jablonka (Cambridge, MA: MIT Press, 2011), pp. 319–30.

Grinker, Roy Richard, *Unstrange Minds: Remapping the World of Autism* (New York: Basic Books, 2008).

Hacking, Ian, 'Humans, Aliens & Autism', *Daedalus*, 138, 3 (2009), 44–59, https://doi.org/10.1162/daed.2009.138.3.44

Hacking, Ian, 'Kinds of People: Moving Targets' in *Proceedings of the British Academy, Volume 151, 2006 Lectures* (Oxford: Oxford University Press/British Academy, 2007), pp. 285–318.

Hacking, Ian, 'The Looping Effects of Human Kinds' in *Causal Cognition*, ed. by Dan Sperber, David Premack, and Ann James Premack (Oxford: Oxford University Press, 1996), pp. 351–83.

Hacking, Ian, *Historical Ontology* (Cambridge, MA: Harvard University Press, 2004).

Hacking, Ian, *The Social Construction of What?* (Cambridge, MA: Harvard University Press, 2001).

Hannah, Laura A. and Steven D. Stagg, 'Experiences of Sex Education and Sexual Awareness in Young Adults with Autism Spectrum Disorder', *Journal of Autism and Developmental Disorders*, 46, 12 (2016), 3678–87, http://doi.org/10.1007/s10803-016-2906-2

Happé, Francesca and Uta Frith, 'The Weak Coherence Account: Detail-Focused Cognitive Style in Autism Spectrum Disorders', *Journal of Autism and Developmental Disorders*, 36 (2006), 5–25, https://doi.org/10.1007/s10803-005-0039-0

Harris, John, 'One Principle and Three Fallacies of Disability Studies', *Journal of Medical Ethics*, 27, 6 (2001), 383–87, http://dx.doi.org/10.1136/jme.27.6.383

Hens, Kristien, 'Dynamiek En Ethiek van de Epigenetica', *Karakter*, 59, (2017).

Hens, Kristien and Raymond Langenberg, 'Immeasurability, Biology, Identity. Citizenship and the Meaning of a Diagnostic Label for Adults Diagnosed with Autism' in *Citizenship in Organizations. Practising the Immeasurable.*, ed. by Suzan Langenberg and Fleur Beyers (London: Palgrave Macmillan, 2017).

Hens, Kristien and Raymond Langenberg, *Experiences of Adults Following an Autism Diagnosis* (Chambersburg: Palgrave Macmillan, 2018).

Hens, Kristien, Hilde Peeters, and Kris Dierickx, 'Genetic Testing and Counseling in the Case of an Autism Diagnosis: A Caregivers Perspective', *European Journal of Medical Genetics*, 59, 9 (2016), 452–58, http://dx.doi.org/10.1016/j.ejmg.2016.08.007

Hens, Kristien, Hilde Peeters, and Kris Dierickx, 'Shooting a Moving Target. Researching Autism Genes: An Interview Study with Professionals', *European Journal of Medical Genetics*, 59, 1 (2016), 32–38, https://doi.org/10.1016/j.ejmg.2015.12.009

Hens, Kristien, Hilde Peeters, and Kris Dierickx, 'The Ethics of Complexity. Genetics and Autism, a Literature Review', *American Journal of Medical Genetics Part B: Neuropsychiatric Genetics*, 171, 3 (2016), https://doi.org/10.1002/ajmg.b.32432

Hens, Kristien, Ilse Noens, Hilde Peeters, and Jean Steyaert, 'The Ethics of Patenting Autism Genes', *Nature Reviews. Genetics*, 19 (2018), 247–48, https://doi.org/10.1038/nrg.2018.17

Hippler, Kathrin and Christian Klicpera, 'A Retrospective Analysis of the Clinical Case Records of "autistic Psychopaths" Diagnosed by Hans Asperger and His Team at the University Children's Hospital, Vienna', *Philosophical Transactions of the Royal Society B: Biological Sciences*, 358 (2003), 291–301, https://doi.org/10.1098/rstb.2002.1197

Hippocrates, *De Morbo Sacro*, Section 1, http://www.perseus.tufts.edu/hopper/text?doc=Perseus%3atext%3a1999.01.0248%3atext%3dMorb.+Sacr. [accessed 18 February 2018].

Hobson, R. Peter, 'Against the Theory of "Theory of Mind"', *British Journal of Developmental Psychology*, 9 (1991), 33–51, https://doi.org/10.1111/j.2044-835X.1991.tb00860.x

Houwen-van Opstal, S. L. S., M. Jansen, N. van Alfen, and I. J. M. de Groot, 'Health-Related Quality of Life and Its Relation to Disease Severity in Boys with Duchenne Muscular Dystrophy: Satisfied Boys, Worrying Parents--a Case-Control Study', *Journal of Child Neurology*, 29, 11 (2014), 1486–95, https://doi.org/10.1177%2F0883073813506490

Huws, Jaci C. and Robert S. P. Jones, 'Diagnosis, Disclosure, and Having Autism: An Interpretative Phenomenological Analysis of the Perceptions of Young People with Autism', *Journal of Intellectual & Developmental Disability*, 33, 2 (2008), 99–107, https://doi.org/10.1080/13668250802010394

Ingersoll, Brooke and Allison Wainer, 'The Broader Autism Phenotype' in *Handbook of Autism and Pervasive Developmental Disorders: Diagnosis, Development, and Brain Mechanisms*, Vol. 1, 4th Ed. (Hoboken, NJ: John Wiley & Sons Inc, 2014), pp. 28–56.

Jaarsma, Pier and Stellan Welin, 'Autism as a Natural Human Variation: Reflections on the Claims of the Neurodiversity Movement', *Health Care Analysis*, 20 (2012), 20–30, https://doi.org/10.1007/s10728-011-0169-9

Jaarsma, Pier and Stellan Welin, 'Human Capabilities, Mild Autism, Deafness and the Morality of Embryo Selection', *Medicine, Health Care and Philosophy: A European Journal*, 16, 4 (2013), 817–24, https://doi.org/10.1007/s11019-013-9464-6

Jacobs, Delphine, Jean Steyaert, Kris Dierickx, and Kristien Hens, 'Parents' views and experiences of the autism spectrum disorder diagnosis of their young child: a longitudinal interview study', *Child and Adolescent Psychiatry*, 29 (2019), 1143–54, https://doi.org/10.1007/s00787-019-01431-4

Jacobs, Delphine, Jean Steyaert, Kris Dierickx, and Kristien Hens, 'Parents' multi-layered expectations when requesting an Autism Spectrum Disorder assessment of their young child: an in-depth interview study', *BMC Psychiatry*, 20 (2020), https://doi.org/10.1186/s12888-020-02806-7

Jacobs, Delphine, Jean Steyaert, Kris Dierickx, and Kristien Hens, 'Physician View and Experience of the Diagnosis of Autism Spectrum Disorder in Young Children', *Frontiers in Psychiatry*, 10 (2019), https://doi.org/10.3389/fpsyt.2019.00372

Jacobs, Delphine, Jean Steyaert, Kris Dierickx, and Kristien Hens, 'Implications of an Autism Spectrum Disorder Diagnosis: An Interview Study of How Physicians Experience the Diagnosis in a Young Child, *Journal of Clinical Medicine*, 7, 10 (2018), https://doi.org/10.3390/jcm7100348

Jaspers, Karl, *General Psychopathology* (Baltimore: JHU Press, 1997).

Jones, Robert S. P., Andrew Zahl, and Jaci C. Huws, 'First-Hand Accounts of Emotional Experiences in Autism: A Qualitative Analysis', *Disability & Society*, 16, 3 (2001), 393–401, https://doi.org/10.1080/09687590120045950

Kafer, Alison, *Feminist, Queer, Crip* (Bloomington: Indiana University Press, 2013).

Kanner, Leo, 'Autistic Disturbances of Affective Contact', *Acta Paedopsychiatrica*, 35, 4 (1968), 100–36.

Kanner, Leo, 'Follow-up Study of Eleven Autistic Children Originally Reported in 1943', *Journal of Autism and Childhood Schizophrenia*, 1 (1971), 119–45, https://doi.org/10.1007/bf01537953

Kanner, Leo, Alejandro Rodriguez, and Barbara Ashenden, 'How Far Can Autistic Children Go in Matters of Social Adaptation?', *Journal of Autism and Childhood Schizophrenia*, 2 (1972), 9–33, https://doi.org/10.1007/BF01537624

Karst, Jeffrey S. and Amy Vaughan Van Hecke, 'Parent and Family Impact of Autism Spectrum Disorders: A Review and Proposed Model for Intervention Evaluation', *Clinical Child and Family Psychology Review*, 15, 3 (2012), 247–77, https://doi.org/10.1007/s10567-012-0119-6

Kennett, Jeanette, 'Autism, Empathy and Moral Agency', *Philosophical Quarterly*, 52, 208 (2002), 340–57, https://doi.org/10.1111/1467-9213.00272

Kenny, Lorcan, Caroline Hattersley, Bonnie Molins, Carole Buckley, Carol Povey, and Elizabeth Pellicano, 'Which Terms Should Be Used to Describe Autism? Perspectives from the UK Autism Community', *Autism*, 20, 4 (2015), 442–62, https://doi.org/10.1177/1362361315588200

Kim, Hyun Uk, 'Autism across Cultures: Rethinking Autism', *Disability & Society*, 27, 4 (2012), 535–45. http://doi.org/10.1080/09687599.2012.659463

Klosin, Adam, Eduard Casas, Cristina Hidalgo-Carcedo, Tanya Vavouri, and Ben Lehner, 'Transgenerational Transmission of Environmental Information in C. Elegans', *Science*, 356 (2017), 320–23, http://doi.org/10.1126/science.aah6412

Lebowitz, Matthew S. and Woo-kyoung Ahn, 'Effects of Biological Explanations for Mental Disorders on Clinicians' Empathy', *Proceedings of the National Academy of Sciences of the United States of America*, 111, 50 (2014), 17786–90, http://doi.org/10.1073/pnas.1414058111

Lemeire, Olivier, 'Soortgelijke stoornissen. Over nut en validiteit van classificatie in de psychiatrie', *Tijdschrift voor Filosofie*, 76, 2 (2014), 217–46, http://doi.org/10.2143/TVF.76.2.3030628

Lucas, P. and A. Sheeran, 'Asperger's Syndrome and the Eccentricity and Genius of Jeremy Bentham', *Journal of Bentham Studies*, 8 (2006), 1–37.

Lundström, Sebastian, Abraham Reichenberg, Henrik Anckarsäter, Paul Lichtenstein, and Christopher Gillberg, 'Autism Phenotype versus Registered Diagnosis in Swedish Children: Prevalence Trends over 10 Years in General Population Samples', *BMJ (Clinical Research Ed.)*, 350 (2015), http://doi.org/10.1136/bmj.h1961

Magiati, Iliana, 'Assessment in Adulthood' in *Handbook of Assessment and Diagnosis of Autism Spectrum Disorder*, ed. by Johnny L. Matson, Autism and Child Psychopathology Series (Chambersburg: Springer International Publishing, 2016), pp. 191–207.

Mandy, William and Meng-Chuan Lai, 'Annual Research Review: The Role of the Environment in the Developmental Psychopathology of Autism Spectrum Condition', *Journal of Child Psychology and Psychiatry, and Allied Disciplines*, 57, 3 (2016), 271–92, http://doi.org/10.1111/jcpp.12501

Markram, Henry, Tania Rinaldi, and Kamila Markram, 'The Intense World Syndrome – an Alternative Hypothesis for Autism', *Frontiers in Neuroscience*, 1 (2007), 77–96, https://doi.org/10.3389/neuro.01.1.1.006.2007

Matson, Johnny L., *Handbook of Assessment and Diagnosis of Autism Spectrum Disorder* (New York: Springer Publishing, 2016).

McCrimmon, Adam and Kristin Rostad, 'Test Review: Autism Diagnostic Observation Schedule, Second Edition (ADOS-2) Manual (Part II): Toddler Module', *Journal of Psychoeducational Assessment*, 32 (2014), 88–92, https://doi.org/10.1177%2F0734282913490916

McGeer, Victoria, 'Autistic Self-Awareness: Comment', *Philosophy, Psychiatry, and Psychology*, 11, 3 (2004), 235–51, https://doi.org/10.1353/ppp.2004.0066

McGeer, Victoria, 'Varieties of Moral Agency: Lessons From Autism (and Psychopathy)' in *Moral Psychology*, Vol. 3, ed. by Walter Sinnott-Armstrong (Cambridge, MA: MIT Press, 2008).

McGuire, Anne and Rod Michalko, 'Minds between Us: Autism, Mindblindness, and the Uncertainty of Communication', *Educational Philosophy and Theory*, 43 (2011), 167–77 https://doi.org/10.1111/j.1469-5812.2009.00537.x

McGuire, Anne, *War on Autism: On the Cultural Logic of Normative Violence* (Ann Arbor, MI: University of Michigan Press, 2016).

Milton, Damian, 'On the ontological status of autism: the 'double empathy problem', *Disability & Society*, 27, 6 (2012), pp. 883-887, https://doi.org/10.1 080/09687599.2012.710008

Miresco, Marc J. and Laurence J. Kirmayer, 'The Persistence of Mind-Brain Dualism in Psychiatric Reasoning about Clinical Scenarios', *The American Journal of Psychiatry*, 163, 5 (2006), 913–18, https://doi.org/10.1176/ajp.2006.163.5.913

Mole, Christopher, 'Autism and "Disease": The Semantics of an Ill-Posed Question', *Philosophical Psychology*, 30 (2017), 1126–40, https://doi.org/10.1 080/09515089.2017.1338341

Mottron, Laurent, *L'intervention précoce pour enfants autistes: Nouveaux principes pour soutenir une autre intelligence* (Brussels: Editions Mardaga, 2016).

Mottron, Laurent, Michelle Dawson, Isabelle Soulières, Benedicte Hubert, and Jake Burack, 'Enhanced Perceptual Functioning in Autism: An Update, and Eight Principles of Autistic Perception', *Journal of Autism and Developmental Disorders*, 36, 1 (2006), 27–43, https://doi.org/10.1007/s10803-005-0040-7

Murray, Dinah, Mike Lesser, and Wendy Lawson, 'Attention, monotropism and the diagnostic criteria for autism', *Autism*, 9, 2 (2005), 139–56, https://doi.org/10.1177%2F1362361305051398

Nadesan, Majia Holmer, 'Autism and Genetics Profit, Risk, and Bare Life' in *Worlds of Autism: Across the Spectrum of Neurological Difference* (Minneapolis: University of Minnesota Press, 2013), pp. 117–42.

Nadesan, Majia Holmer, *Constructing Autism: Unravelling the 'Truth' and Understanding the Social* (London; New York: Routledge, 2005).

Navon, Daniel and Gil Eyal, 'Looping Genomes: Diagnostic Change and the Genetic Makeup of the Autism Population', *AJS; American Journal of Sociology*, 121, 5 (2016), 1416–71, https://doi.org/10.1086/684201

Nelkin, Dorothy and M. Susan Lindee, *The DNA Mystique: The Gene as a Cultural Icon* (Ann Arbor, MI: University of Michigan, 2004).

Noens, Ilse, Herbert Roeyers, Cis Schiltmans, Hanna Steenwegen, Jean Steyaert, and Peter Vermeulen, 'Naar Een Autismevriendelijk Vlaanderen. Aanbevelingen van de Taskforce Autisme in Opdracht van Minister Jo Vandeurzen', (2016).

Norbury, Courtenay Frazier and Alison Sparks, 'Difference or Disorder? Cultural Issues in Understanding Neurodevelopmental Disorders', *Developmental Psychology*, 49, 1 (2013), 45–58, https://doi.org/10.1037/a0027446

Ortega, Francisco, Rafaela Zorzanelli, and Clarice Rios, 'The Biopolitics of Autism in Brazil' in *Re-Thinking Autism. Diagnosis, Identity and Equality*, ed. by Katherine Runswick-Cole, Rebecca Mallett, and Sami Timimi (London and Philadelphia: Jessica Kingsley Publishers, 2016), p. 19.

Patil, Indrajeet, Jens Melsbach, Kristina Hennig-Fast, and Giorgia Silani, 'Divergent Roles of Autistic and Alexithymic Traits in Utilitarian Moral Judgments in Adults with Autism', *Scientific Reports*, 6 (2016), https://doi.org/10.1038/srep23637

Pembrey, Marcus E., Lars Olov Bygren, Gunnar Kaati, Soren Edvinsson, Kate Northstone, Michael Sjostrom, Jean Golding, and the ALSPAC Study Team, 'Sex-Specific, Male-Line Transgenerational Responses in Humans', *European Journal of Human Genetics*, 14 (2005), 159–66, https://doi.org/10.1038/sj.ejhg.5201538

Penrose, Roger, Abner Shimony, Nancy Cartwright, and Stephen Hawking, *The Large, the Small and the Human Mind* (Cambridge: Cambridge University Press, 2000).

Pentzell, Nick, 'I Think, Therefore I Am. I Am Verbal, Therefore I Live.' in *The Philosophy of Autism*, ed. by Jami L. Anderson and Simon Cushing (Lanham: Rowman & Littlefield, 2013), pp. 103–8.

Peterson, Candida C., Virginia Slaughter, James Peterson, and David Premack, 'Children with Autism Can Track Others' Beliefs in a Competitive Game',

Developmental Science, 16, 3 (2013), 443–50, https://doi.org/10.1111/desc.12040

Premack, David and G. Woodruff, 'Does the Chimpanzee Have a Theory of Mind?', *Behavioural and Brain Sciences*, 4 (1978), 515–629.

Richardson, Sarah S., Cynthia R. Daniels, Matthew W. Gillman, Janet Golden, Rebecca Kukla, Christopher Kuzawa, and others, 'Society: Don't Blame the Mothers', *Nature*, 512 (2014), 131–32, https://doi.org/10.1038/512131a

Richman, Kenneth and Raya Bidshahri, 'Autism, Theory of Mind, and the Reactive Attitudes', *Bioethics*, 32, 1 (2017), pp. 43–49, https://doi.org/10.1111/bioe.12370

Rimland, Bernard, *Infantile Autism: The Syndrome and Its Implications for a Neural Theory of behaviour* (Methuen, MA: Methuen Publishing, 1964).

Rodogno, Raffaele, Katrine Krause-Jensen, and Richard E. Ashcroft, 'Autism and the Good Life: A New Approach to the Study of Well-Being', *Journal of Medical Ethics*, 42 (2016), 401–8, http://doi.org/10.1136/medethics-2016-103595

Rose, Nikolas and Joelle M. Abi-Rached, *Neuro: The New Brain Sciences and the Management of the Mind* (Princeton: Princeton University Press, 2013).

Rose, Nikolas, *Inventing Our Selves: Psychology, Power, and Personhood* (Cambridge: Cambridge University Press, 1998).

Russell, James, *Autism as an Executive Disorder* (Oxford: Oxford University Press, 1997).

Ryle, Gilbert, *The Concept of Mind* (Chicago: University of Chicago Press, 1949).

Sarrett, Jennifer C., 'Biocertification and Neurodiversity: The Role and Implications of Self-Diagnosis in Autistic Communities', *Neuroethics*, 9 (2016), 23–36, https://doi.org/10.1007/s12152-016-9247-x

Savulescu, Julian, 'Procreative Beneficence: Why We Should Select the Best Children', *Bioethics*, 15 (2001), 413–26, https://doi.org/10.1111/1467-8519.00251

Savulescu, Julian and Guy Kahane, 'The Moral Obligation to Create Children with the Best Chance of the Best Life', *Bioethics*, 23, 5 (2009), 274–90, https://doi.org/10.1111/j.1467-8519.2008.00687.x

Schriber, Roberta A., Richard W. Robins, and Marjorie Solomon, 'Personality and Self-Insight in Individuals with Autism Spectrum Disorder', *Journal of Personality and Social Psychology*, 106, 1 (2014), 112–30, https://doi.org/10.1037/a0034950

Strawson, P.F., 'Freedom and Resentment', *Proceedings of the British Academy*, 48, 1 (1962), 1–25, https://doi.org/10.1073/pnas.48.1.1

Swaab, Dick, *Wij zijn ons brein: van baarmoeder tot Alzheimer* (London: Atlas Contact, 2010).

Scully, Jackie Leach, 'The Convention on the Rights of Persons with Disabilities and Cultural Understandings of Disability' in *Disability and Universal Human Rights: Legal, Ethical and Conceptual Implications of the Convention on the Rights of Persons with Disabilities*, ed. by Joel Anderson and Jos Philips (Utrecht: Netherlands Institute of Human Rights (SIM), 2012), pp. 71–83.

Scully, Jackie Leach, *Disability Bioethics: Moral Bodies, Moral Difference* (Plymouth: Rowman & Littlefield, 2008).

Sholl, Jonathan, 'Escaping the Conceptual Analysis Straitjacket: Pathological Mechanisms and Canguilhem's Biological Philosophy', *Perspectives in Biology and Medicine*, 58 (2015), 395–418, https://doi.org/10.1353/pbm.2015.0032

Silberman, Steve, *NeuroTribes: The Legacy of Autism and How to Think Smarter About People Who Think Differently* (Sydney: Allen & Unwin, 2015).

Silverman, Chloe, *Understanding Autism: Parents, Doctors, and the History of a Disorder* (Princeton: Princeton University Press, 2011)

Sinha, Pawan, Margaret M. Kjelgaard, Tapan K. Gandhi, Kleovoulos Tsourides, Annie L. Cardinaux, Dimitrios Pantazis, and others, 'Autism as a Disorder of Prediction', *Proceedings of the National Academy of Sciences*, 111, 42 (2014), 15220–25, https://doi.org/10.1073/pnas.1416797111

Skotko, Brian G. and Susan P. Levine, 'What the Other Children Are Thinking: Brothers and Sisters of Persons with Down Syndrome', *American Journal of Medical Genetics. Part C, Seminars in Medical Genetics*, 142 (2006), 180–86.

Skotko, Brian G., Susan P. Levine, and Richard Goldstein, 'Having a Son or Daughter with Down Syndrome: Perspectives from Mothers and Fathers', *American Journal of Medical Genetics. Part A*, 155, 10 (2011), 2335–47, https://doi.org/10.1002/ajmg.a.34293

Skotko, Brian G., Susan P. Levine, and Richard Goldstein, 'Self-Perceptions from People with Down Syndrome', *American Journal of Medical Genetics. Part A*, 155 (2011), 2360–69, https://doi.org/10.1002/ajmg.a.34235

Smith, Adam, 'The Empathy Imbalance Hypothesis of Autism: A Theoretical Approach to Cognitive and Emotional Empathy in Autistic Development', *Psychological Record*, 59 (2009), 489–510, https://doi.org/10.1007/BF03395675

Smith, Jonathan, *Interpretative Phenomenological Analysis: Theory, Method and Research*, First edition (Los Angeles: SAGE Publications Ltd, 2009).

Thompson, Evan, *Mind in Life: Biology, Phenomenology, and the Sciences of Mind* (Cambridge, MA: Harvard University Press, 2007).

Tijdschrift Voor Psychiatrie, *Diagnostic and Statistical Manual of Mental Disorders (5de Druk)*, Vol. 5 (2013), http://www.tijdschriftvoorpsychiatrie.nl/en/issues/472/articles/10181 [accessed 18 February 2018].

Timimi, Sami, 'Children's Mental Health: Time to Stop Using Psychiatric Diagnosis', *European Journal of Psychotherapy & Counselling*, 17, 4 (2015), 342–58, https://doi.org/10.1080/13642537.2015.1094500

Timimi, Sami, Neil Gardner, and Brian McCabe, *The Myth of Autism: Medicalising Men's and Boys' Social and Emotional Competence* (London: Macmillan Education UK, 2010).

Tomasello, Michael and Carpenter Malinda, 'Shared Intentionality', *Developmental Science*, 10, 1 (2006), 121–25, https://doi.org/10.1111/j.1467-7687.2007.00573.x

Trembath, David, Carmela Germano, Graeme Johanson, and Cheryl Dissanayake, 'The Experience of Anxiety in Young Adults With Autism Spectrum Disorders', *Focus on Autism and Other Developmental Disabilities*, 27, 4 (2012), 213–24, https://doi.org/10.1177/1088357612454916

Van de Cruys, Sander, Kris Evers, Ruth Van der Hallen, Lien Van Eylen, Bart Boets, Lee de-Wit, and others, 'Precise Minds in Uncertain Worlds: Predictive Coding in Autism', *Psychological Review*, 121, 4 (2014), 649–75, https://doi.org/10.1037/a0037665

Van Goidsenhoven, Leni, *Autisme in veelvoud: het potentieel van life writing voor alternatieve vormen van subjectiviteit.* (Antwerp: Maklu-Uitgevers, 2020).

Van Grunsven Janna, 'Perceiving 'Other' Minds: Autism, 4E Cognition, and the Idea of Neurodiversity', *The Journal of Consciousness Studies*, 27, 7-8 (2020), 115-143.

Verbeke, Evi, 'Diagnoses als mogelijke decompenserende factor', *Tijdschrift voor Psychoanalyse*, 22, 4 (2016), 283–93.

Verhoeff, Berend, 'Autism in Flux: A History of the Concept from Leo Kanner to DSM-5', *History of Psychiatry*, 24, 4 (2013), 442–58, https://doi.org/10.1177%2F0957154X13500584

Verhoeff, Berend, 'Michel Foucault Voorbij Antipsychiatrie: Macht, Vrijheid En de Mens in de Maak' in *Handboek Psychiatrie En Filosofie* (Utrecht: de Tijdstroom, 2012), pp. 69–81.

Verhoeff, Berend, 'Fundamental Challenges for Autism Research: The Science-Practice Gap, Demarcating Autism and the Unsuccessful Search for the Neurobiological Basis of Autism', *Medicine, Health Care, and Philosophy*, 18 (2015), 443–47, https://doi.org/10.1007/s11019-015-9636-7

Verhoeff, Berend, 'The Autism Puzzle: Challenging a Mechanistic Model on Conceptual and Historical Grounds', *Philosophy, Ethics, and Humanities in Medicine*, 8, 17 (2013), https://doi.org/10.1186/1747-5341-8-17

Wakefield, Jerome C., 'The Concept of Mental Disorder: Diagnostic Implications of the Harmful Dysfunction Analysis', *World Psychiatry*, 6, 3 (2007), 149–56.

Waltz, Mitzi, *Autism. A Social and Medical History* (Hampshire: Palgrave McMillan, 2013).

Waterhouse, Lynn, Eric London, and Christopher Gillberg, 'ASD Validity', *Review Journal of Autism and Developmental Disorders*, 3 (2016), 1–28, https://doi.org/10.1007/s40489-016-0085-x

Waterhouse, Lynn, *Rethinking Autism: Variation and Complexity* (Cambridge, MA: Academic Press, 2013).

West, John, Graham Douglas, Stephen Houghton, Vivienne Lawrence, Ken Whiting, and Ken Glasgow, 'Time Perception in Boys with Attention-Deficit/ Hyperactivity Disorder According to Time Duration, Distraction and Mode of Presentation', *Child Neuropsychology: A Journal on Normal and Abnormal Development in Childhood and Adolescence*, 6, 4 (2000), 241–50, https://doi. org/10.1076/chin.6.4.241.3140

Whitelaw, Emma, 'Epigenetics: Sins of the Fathers, and Their Fathers', *European Journal of Human Genetics*, 14 (2006), 131–32, https://doi.org/10.1038/ sj.ejhg.5201567

Williams, David, 'Theory of Own Mind in Autism Evidence of a Specific Deficit in Self-Awareness?', *Autism*, 14, 5 (2010), 474–94, https://doi. org/10.1177%2F1362361310366314

Wing, Lorna, 'Asperger's Syndrome: A Clinical Account', *Psychological Medicine*, 11 (1981), 115–29, https://doi.org/10.1017/S0033291700053332

Wiorkowski, Fleur, 'The Experiences of Students with Autism Spectrum Disorders in College: A Heuristic Exploration', *The Qualitative Report*, 20, 6 (2015), 847, https://doi.org/10.46743/2160-3715/2015.2163

Yergeau, Melanie, and Bryce Huebner, 'Minding Theory of Mind', *Journal of Social Philosophy*, 48, 3 (2017), 273–96, https://doi.org/10.1111/josp.12191

Index

About the Team

Alessandra Tosi was the managing editor for this book.

Lucy Barnes performed the copy-editing and proofreading.

Anna Gatti designed the cover. The cover was produced in InDesign using the Fontin font.

Luca Baffa typeset the book in InDesign and produced the paperback and hardback editions. The text font is Tex Gyre Pagella; the heading font is Californian FB. Luca produced the EPUB, MOBI, PDF, HTML, and XML editions — the conversion is performed with open source software freely available on our GitHub page (https://github.com/OpenBookPublishers).

This book need not end here...

Share

All our books — including the one you have just read — are free to access online so that students, researchers and members of the public who can't afford a printed edition will have access to the same ideas. This title will be accessed online by hundreds of readers each month across the globe: why not share the link so that someone you know is one of them?

This book and additional content is available at:

https://doi.org/10.11647/OBP.0261

Customise

Personalise your copy of this book or design new books using OBP and third-party material. Take chapters or whole books from our published list and make a special edition, a new anthology or an illuminating coursepack. Each customised edition will be produced as a paperback and a downloadable PDF.

Find out more at:

https://www.openbookpublishers.com/section/59/1

9 781800 642317